GIFTS

Girls In Fellowship And Team Study

By Hannah Giselbach

Second Edition

While this book is for all teenage women, it also accompanies the GIFTS program for spiritual leadership development, part of Lads to Leaders. For more information about GIFTS (including rules for participation) and Lads to Leaders, please visit www.lads-to-leaders.org.

Preface

Ah…the life of a teenage girl…so crazy and yet so wonderful. These few years between girlhood and womanhood are truly amazing. The decisions we make right now are ones that will affect our entire lives. So much of what happens in our lives will depend on the choices we make today.

This is all very exciting, but at the same time, frightening and overwhelming. We're being pressured by so many different sources. We're suddenly discovering things about life that we never have before. We're forced to no longer believe whatever our parents believe but to develop our own beliefs and opinions.

So, what's the most important thing to remember in this amazing adventure of growing up? If I could leave you with just one thought after reading this book, it would be this: In 100 years, it won't matter if I bought my clothes from American Eagle. It won't matter if I was popular in high school. It won't matter if I saw all the latest movies. The only thing that will matter is that I was faithful Christian. True success is simply living my life and going to heaven.

This book is called G.I.F.T.S.. It's an acronym for "Girls In Fellowship And Team Study," but it has a double meaning. It also references the gifts, or talents, that each one of us possesses for the purpose of glorifying God. May God bless you as you use your gifts to reach that awesome goal! I hope that studying this book will help you to do that.

~Hannah

Table of Contents

CHAPTER ONE:
What's Love Got To Do With It?

I adore acting. It has always been one my favorite hobbies. The other day I was running around my room getting ready to go somewhere, when I turned on the radio and heard a very important message. A prestigious casting director was coming to Huntsville to allow teenagers to audition for a part in a popular children's sitcom. I was thrilled. This just might be the big break for me. I immediately dropped what I was doing and called the number which was announced several times (you know, just in case you didn't write it down the first time). I sat and listened to several minutes of elevator music until someone was finally able to speak with me. I heard an energetic "hello." I told the lady that I wanted to audition for the show, and she wrote down my address, phone number, age, etc., and then told me I would be performing before a camera. After reminding me to bring a headshot as well as a full-length shot, she wished me good luck and then hung up the phone. I couldn't wait. I went right to the closet to decide what to wear. My audition was at 1:30 on Sunday afternoon.

After worship on Sunday, Mom took me to a Mexican restaurant (the best way to eat!), but I had trouble enjoying it on account of my nerves. When we arrived at the audition location, I was amazed at the number of teenagers, like myself, who were already there. The place was packed with starry-eyed girls and guys who were ready to make their dreams realities. I took a vacant seat near the back. They gave us this long pep talk about success and making something of ourselves. What puzzled me was that they only mentioned the audition once. The rest was about modeling. I suddenly realized that this whole thing about being on TV could possibly just be a front to get our money. I turned to Mom and whispered, "Is this real?" She was just as skeptical as I was. It shocked me when they asked the crowd, "What is true success?" The unanimous answer was, "Money." I have always been taught that true success is living your life and going to heaven. It hurt me to hear their sad and confused opinion.

It turned out that I was right about them just using television auditions as bait to get us there. They packed us in there like sardines just to convince us that we would be "extremely privileged if we were one of the ones chosen" to pay $2000 to have them teach us how to be great models for their modeling agency (yeah, right).

How was I to know they weren't for real? It sure sounded wonderful.

We're all faced with the question "What is real?" at one point or another. This chapter will help you find the answer in regard to spiritual matters.

Is God Real?

Did you know that there is a big fish in the ocean that gets his teeth cleaned by a little fish? After spending the day feeding on little fish, the Oriental Sweetlips (gotta love that name!) decides it's time to get his teeth cleaned. To do this, he looks for a particular type of coral where the Blue-Streak Wrasse lives. When he finds that coral, he swims up to it with his mouth wide open, at which time the Blue Streak Wrasse darts out of the coral and directly into the mouth of the Oriental Sweetlips. This little fish then proceeds to eat all of the food remains off of the Oriental Sweetlips' teeth. This is the main food source for the Blue Streak Wrasse (and you thought the Atkins diet was gross!). If it were not for the Oriental Sweetlips, the Blue Streak Wrasse would starve to death. What's even more amazing is that the Oriental Sweetlips knows not to chomp down on the Blue-Streak Wrasse when it finishes its work. Sweetlips allows the little fish to swim back into the coral so that he can have his teeth cleaned again tomorrow. If it were not for the Blue Streak Wrasse, God's dental hygienist to Mr. Lips, the Oriental Sweetlips' teeth would rot, and therefore, he would starve to death. Is that cool or what?

Did you know that the blind shrimp has a live-in "seeing-eye fish?" The blind shrimp and the goby live in most tropical seas, and are always found together. They live in a hole on the ocean floor that has been dug by the blind shrimp. Ocean currents are constantly throwing debris into the hole, so the shrimp has an almost non-stop job of clearing out the debris. As the name implies, the blind shrimp cannot see, so he is always in danger. He has no way of knowing when predators are nearing the hole. This is where the goby comes in.

The goby has perfect vision. When the shrimp has to clear out the debris from the hole, the goby goes out with it. While the shrimp digs, the goby keeps watch. The shrimp keeps one of his feelers on the goby while he is digging. If the goby sees a predator, he signals by flicking his tail, and they both dart back into the hole at lightning speed. Since the hole is too small for predators, they are both protected from danger. The goby, God's 24 hour watchman and alarm system for the blind shrimp, would not have protection if it were not for the hole built by the blind shrimp. That makes the blind shrimp somewhat of a landlord, and the goby pays his rent by being the trusting watchman. Is that cool or what?!

Did you know that if the earth were only 10% closer to the sun, we would all burn up in fire? Did you know that if we were only 10% further away from the sun, we would all freeze to death? Is that cool or what? No, that's freezing! ∫

Studying amazing scientific facts and phenomena should give you a great appreciation for the power and ingenuity of a Higher Being. The examples I gave you are only glimpses into the stunning universe. I am in awe when I think that the half has never even been told. While scientists are daily finding new evidences of intricate design in our universe, with each newly found phenomenon, the main discovery seems to be that there's so much left to discover!

It's up to each of us to weigh the evidence of our ordered universe, and it isn't weighing the evidence if you only study school textbooks written by atheists. You must also find evidences from leaders in the scientific community who have spent years doing their own scientific research, discovering that there is a Higher Being that created this universe. One such science "think tank" is Apologetics Press. AP produces awesome faith-building tools such as the Apologetics Press Christian Evidences Correspondence Course, Reason and Revelation, and Discovery Magazine. One Apologetics Press author, Kyle Butt, has written a wonderful book entitled, "Is the Bible from God?" which I highly recommend. Be sure to check at the end of this chapter for ordering information. I can promise you that your faith will develop beautifully as you use all of these spiritual and scientific aids and as you discover that the very idea that all of creation simply "popped into existence" or evolved from nothing is absolutely absurd. Every design must have a designer. If I go to a fashion show, I know that the clothes people are wearing on the runway were designed by someone. They didn't just evolve. Someone spent hours designing and creating the outfits. If this is true with one little outfit, don't you think the same would apply in regard to this intricate universe of which we are a part? I beg you to study evidences of creation so that you will know how to respond when your peers try to convince you that God is a myth. You will learn about many flaws in the theory of evolution that your science teachers may fail to mention. Before you move on to any of the moral issues this book will cover, you must be sure that there really is a God, and that there really is an eternal dwelling place, and that the way you choose to live your life now will determine where you will spend eternity.

Do I Want To Serve Him?

After you establish the fact that there is a God, you must decide whether or not you wish to dedicate your life to serving Him.

As a growing Christian girl, I admit that probably the primary reason I'm doing it is out of fear. I know that if I choose not to let God take complete control of every area of my life, I will not go to heaven. Instead I will spend a never-ending eternity burning in fire hotter than any fire we have on earth. I know that I will be there grinding my teeth because of the pain and there will be no relief. Matthew 24:50-51 says, "The Lord of that servant shall come in a day when he looketh not for him, and in an hour that he is not aware of, and shall cut him asunder, and appoint him his portion with the hypocrites: there shall be weeping and gnashing of teeth."

Heaven will be more beautiful than anything we can imagine, which should be enough to make us want to go there, but the alternative should terrify us. I really cannot fathom having to spend one minute in and among the terrors of hell, much less eternity.

The opposite of hell should be an awesome motivation for us, as well. I can't wait to go to heaven and meet great people of faith praised for their righteousness in the Bible. I want to see Jesus, and thank Him, again and again, for what He's done for me. I want to touch the face of God. I want to see my grandmother, and other relatives and friends waiting there for me. I want to walk the streets of gold and enjoy the royalty and majesty that will surround me.

Revelation 21:4 says, "And God shall wipe away all tears from their eyes; and there shall be no more death, neither sorrow, nor crying, neither shall there be anymore pain…" Isn't that sweet? That's a happiness that no one on earth has ever experienced. I would love to feel that complete and ecstatic bliss which is promised.

Besides fear of punishment and our longing for heaven, we should want to serve Him because of what He did for us. Jesus left a place that was truly perfect (with no sin, no sadness, no pain, and no death) to come to this sinful, wicked world. Why? Because there was only one sacrifice that could be made to erase sin in this world (Hebrews 10:4, 9-12). He had to go through extreme persecution and agony. He was beaten and hung on a wooden cross with nails going through one side of His hands and feet and right out the other. While on the cross, he had to lift His entire body weight up with his pierced hands every time he needed to draw a breath. Besides all the physical torture he had to endure, he was also ridiculed to the extreme. The people made a crown of sharp thorns and mashed it down on His head. They put a royal robe on Him, spit on Him, and mocked Him. When I imagine the people bowing down and yelling, "Hail, King of the Jews," (Matthew 27:29) at Him between laughs, it absolutely infuriates me. Jesus is perfect in every way. He is God. He created those people, and yet, in spite of all of that, they spat on Him and called Him names.

Knowing that if I were the only person on earth, He would have done it all anyway, just for me, makes me want to give Him something in return. All I have to do is love Him, fully and totally. If I love Him that much, I will obey His commands and sacrifice all sinful pleasures to please Him (John 14:23).

Another reason I have the earnest desire to serve Him is because He is the only one who knows me inside and out, and who knows exactly what is best for me. He promised that if I love and obey Him, He will work things out for my ultimate benefit (Romans 8:28). I don't ever have to worry. He's going to make something good come from each heartache that I face, whether it is great or small. Just knowing that He'll help me get through any problems I face motivates me to put myself in full submission to Him. Life's tough. Who wants to go through it all alone?

Commit!

Once you establish in your heart that there is a God, and that you do want to serve Him, you must donate every single part of your life to Him. Allow Him to take over everything that you do. This doesn't mean you can't have fun anymore, but it may mean giving up some activities you enjoy. Matthew 6:33 says, "...Seek ye first the kingdom of God, and His righteousness...." That means we're to make Christ our first priority. It means that, in my study, if I discover that I'm not doing something God wants me to do, I'll do it. If I discover that I'm doing something God doesn't want me to do, I'll stop doing it. I understand that this is so much easier said than done, but God never said the Christian life would be easy. We won't just happen to be faithful Christians. It takes lots of time and effort.

On the next page is a pledge promising your commitment. Please sign it only if you plan to abide by it. I want this to be a promise you'll re-member yourself making as you face all of the temptations this life holds.

My Pledge

I, _____ promise to study God's word as I read this book with an open heart to what God has to say. I promise to sacrifice whatever I must in order to be in full accordance with His Will. I promise to "roll up my sleeves" and start doing the things He wants me to do for Him. I promise not to forget this pledge I have made as I read the remaining chapters of this book, and as I make moral decisions in this life.

Signed_____

Witness_____

(Beside "Witness" have your Bible class teacher, a parent, or a faithful Christian sign. This witness can help you remember what's most important when you face temptation or difficult days.)

If you signed the pledge, I know we'll have an awesome study of God's Word as we continue through the pages of this book.

Works Cited

Dr. Jay L. Wile and Marilyn F. Durnell, Exploring Creation with Biology (Chelsea: Sheridan Books, Inc., 1998), pp. 318-319

Ibid p. 317

Bert Thompson, Ph.D. and Kyle Butt, M.A., Apologetics Press Christian Evidences Correspondence Course

Ordering Information for Apologetics Press materials:
    203 Landmark Drive,
    Montgomery, Alabama
    36117
    (334)272-8558
    www.ApologeticsPress.org

Ordering Information for Apologia Educational Ministries Curriculum Support (Hannah's 9th grade Biology book):
    Dr. Jay L. Wile
    Apologia Educational Ministries, Inc.
    1106 Meridian Plaza, Suite 220
    Anderson, IN
    46016
    (765)608-3280
    www.highschoolscience.com

Questions:

1. What are some other awesome and amazing examples of creation that declare God as a living being?

2. Name some reasons that we should want to serve the Lord.

3. Is it okay to serve God because of fear? Can you offer scriptures to support your answer?

4. Discuss personal reasons you look forward to heaven.

5. Make a list of verses that describe heaven. Read and discuss these together.

6. Make a list of things that will be in heaven. On the opposite side of the page, make a list of things that will not be in heaven.

7. What are some activities that new-born Christians may need to give up in order to please God?

Projects

Choose an animal, research its anatomy and characteristics. Write a 500 word research paper on its amazing design and present this paper to your study group.

Do some research and find a great scientist who believes or believed in God. Write a 300 word report on his/her life. Be sure to credit your sources!

Visit www.apologeticspress.org and read five articles evidencing the existence of a higher being.

Order and complete the introductory level Christian Evidences Correspondence Course from Apologetics Press. The address, phone number, and email address, for AP is in this chapter.

Subscribe to Discovery Magazine or Reason and Revelation for one year and commit to reading each issue you receive.

CHAPTER TWO:
No Turning Back

"So then faith comes by hearing, and hearing by the word of God" (Romans 10:17).

This chapter will cover our faithfulness to Christ. What is faith? Faith, simply put, is a confident belief in the trustworthiness of God. In other words, if God said it, I believe it. I'm reminded of when I was little, maybe three or four years old, and my brother, Caleb, and I would stand on something too high to jump to the ground, so my dad would stand below us to catch us. Daddy would notice my hesitancy in jumping, and say, "Hannah, do you believe I can catch you?" I would reply, "Of course I do, Daddy!" Then he would say, "Then jump!" I would then say, "I just want Caleb to go first." I believed he could catch me, but my faith wasn't strong enough for me to act on that faith. Real faith is believing in God and serving Him wholeheartedly even though we can't see Him. We have to trust that He'll keep His promises to us.

BY FAITH (Hebrews 11:1)

Hebrews 11 is known as the "Hall of Faith" because of the many faithful people mentioned in this chapter. It describes wonderful and amazing things these people did, all "by faith." They all obviously put a lot of emphasis on their spirituality.

There are two ways people look at their Christianity. The first way is to look at life like a giant pie divided into several different slices, each representing what we do with our time. One slice would represent my family; another, my friends. One might be my choices of entertainment and another would be schoolwork. You get the idea. One piece is my Christianity; that is, the time I spend studying my Bible, praying, and worshipping. When you finish labeling all the pieces of your pie, the picture looks pretty complete, right? Actually this is the wrong way to view our lives.

The right way is this: This time picture an old fashioned wagon wheel. In this illustration my time is represented by the spokes of that wheel. One spoke is my job. Another is the time I spend at school, and so on. The hub of this wheel is Jesus Christ. None of the spokes move unless the hub moves. Every spoke is connected to the hub. Why is this better than the pie?

Well, you see, in the pie illustration, if I were to remove the "Christ" piece of the pie, all of the other pieces would remain unaltered. They would stay the same. However, if you were to take the hub out of the wheel, the rest of the wheel would fall apart. It has to have the hub to be of any use at all. Each spoke (i.e. area of my life) is fully dependent on Christ. The hub rules!

As in the previous chapter, look at Matthew 6:33, "Seek ye first the kingdom of God, and his righteousness, and all these things shall be added unto you." That means that our Christianity has to be the most important thing to us; the "hub" of our lives.

Biblical Examples of Faithfulness

Of course, there are too many examples of faithfulness in the Bible for me to cover in this chapter, so I'll just touch on a few which have inspired me personally.

In Daniel 6 we read a familiar story about Daniel's faith. King Darius had signed the decree that anyone who asked a petition of any god or man besides the king would be thrown into a den of hungry lions. At this point, Daniel certainly could have just prayed inside his house with the windows shut and no one would know. This would have been convenient and safe. However, verse 10 reads, "Now when Daniel knew that the writing was signed, he went into his house, and his windows being open in his chamber toward Jerusalem, he kneeled upon his knees three times a day, and prayed, and gave thanks before his God, as he did aforetime."

So, Daniel made a life-endangering statement about his faith in the one true God. Of course, there would have been nothing wrong with Daniel praying alone and out of sight, but his custom was to kneel in prayer three times a day, with his windows open. He refused to allow any man's decree to prevent him from talking to God without shame or secrecy. We see in verse 22 that God delivered Daniel from the mouths of the blood-thirsty lions.

In Daniel 3 we read about some of Daniel's friends; Shadrach, Meshach, and Abednego. Nebuchadnezzar, the king at that time, had commanded "all people, nations, and languages" to bow down before the statue which Nebuchadnezzar had created. We read of the three faithful men vehemently refusing to obey this command in verses 16-18. I imagine thousands of people falling on their faces, perfectly in sync, when the music began...all except three. I'm sure it wasn't difficult to notice these three brave soldiers standing tall in the midst of a sea of prostrate Nebuchadnezzar yes-men. It would have been so much simpler just to get on their knees, perhaps while whispering prayers of devotion and praise to the one true, living God. However, these men chose to make a statement before these thousands, and before a king who supposedly had the power to destroy every one of them. It gives me chills to imagine them looking King Nebuchadnezzar square in the eyes and saying, "...We are not careful to answer you in this matter. If it be so, our God whom we serve is able to deliver us from the burning fiery furnace, and he will deliver us out of thine hand, oh king," (Daniel 3:16,17).

They didn't say, "Give us five minutes to discuss this, and we'll give you an answer shortly." They didn't need to have a conference. They didn't need to call their parents. They didn't delay for even a second in answering the wicked king. It is obvious that these guys had faith to move mountains.

As the king had warned, Shadrach, Meshach, and Abednego were thrown into a fiery furnace. However, God delivered them from even being touched by the flames (Daniel 3:27). Their faithfulness protected them from peril.

The book of Job tells the story of a man whose faith was put to the test in the greatest sense of the word. Job 1:2-4 describes Job's wealth in detail. Satan told God that Job was faithful only because God had blessed him so richly (verses 9-11). To prove Job's faithfulness, God took away everything Job had at once. Job was very sad, but not discouraged (verses 21, 22). He fell down on his face and, in spite of his hardships, proclaimed, "The Lord gave and the Lord hath taken away. Blessed be the name of the Lord." Verse 22 reads, "In all this, Job sinned not, nor charged God foolishly."

And so it seems Satan was wrong. Game over. Try again. But Satan didn't give up (he never does!). Satan said (and I'm paraphrasing), "Okay, God, maybe he's stronger than I thought, but take away his health and put him in a lot of pain, and he'll curse you to your face." God replied, "Behold, he is in thine hand, but save his life," (Job 2:6). In other words, "Do what you will, but don't kill him."

Job's pain and affliction was immense (2:7-8), but he still continued to praise God for His goodness. His own wife tried to persuade him to curse God so that he would die (at least that's what she thought would happen), but Job triumphantly replied in Job 2:10, "...Thou speakest as one of the foolish women speaketh. What? Shall we receive good at the hand of God, and shall we not receive evil?' In all this did not Job sin with his lips." We all know the rest of the story. Job remained faithful and God blessed him with twice as much as he had before (Job 42:10-17).

All of these examples demonstrate the blessings that go along with faithfulness.

A Good Barometer Of Faithfulness

Now let's take time for a little reflection. What are our attendance patterns in worship services and Bible classes? You may say, "Oh, I attend almost all the time. I hardly ever miss. It has to be a BIG tournament or a BIG test the next day, or I have to be REALLY tired if I don't get up for church every Sunday."

All these seem like reasonable excuses, right? Not really. Do you realize what you're saying? Whether you mean to or not, you're saying big ball games, schoolwork, and enough sleep is more important than worshipping God! It's so easy to get caught up in our busy schedules without taking the time to worship faithfully. But, remember, every time you miss worship for any other activity, you're making it easier to skip church the next time you're really busy. This continues to occur until it doesn't even bother your conscience to miss. Eventually you'll find yourself saying, "When was the last time I went to church?" Satan works discreetly, so when you realize you've lost that number-one priority, it may come as a shock to you.

Staying faithful is no easy task. It means sacrifice. I know a girl who was given an important role in a community theater play. From the get-go, even when auditioning, she told her directors that she would not be present for an hour each night during dress rehearsals for four straight nights of rehearsal. Her reason for this was that the gospel meeting was during dress rehearsal that week, and she would not put theater or any other activity in front of worshipping God. The directors said, "OK," so she was given a role in the play. When her mother came to pick her up on a Tuesday night 10 minutes before the service began that night, her director was, shall we say...less than thrilled, especially because the girl had to leave in the middle of an important scene to go to worship.

That night, the girl was touched by the lesson, and became a Christian by putting on Christ in baptism. She came back late and with damp hair, and had the opportunity to answer her friends' questions by telling them the reason for baptism, and the difference Christ had made in her life.

Another example comes to mind of a girl who was given the opportunity to go on a 3-day school trip to New York City. One of her life-long dreams was to visit the Big Apple. Before she agreed to go, she asked the question about worship. She was told that they would only be there Thursday, Friday, and Saturday, not missing any services. Thrilled out of her mind, the girl worked hard for the few months she had before the trip. She finally saved up enough to go, and it was only a few more weeks before departure. Everything changed, however, when the girl overheard someone discussing the flight home...on Sunday!

Surely there's been a mistake, the girl said to herself. She called the teacher and supervisor of the trip and was informed that the plans had been changed, and the group would be visiting the Statue of Liberty on Sunday morning before flying home. The girl asked if she could be excused for a couple of hours that day to find a place to worship. "I'm sorry, but no," was the answer. The money she had deposited was non-refundable, and another girl got an almost free trip to New York because of this girl's priorities. You see, attendance is not the whole of faithfulness, but it is a good barometer of faith. Our attendance patterns reflect what our priorities are.

True faithfulness means sacrifice, but it's an essential part of salvation. Remember, as you look back on your life one day, you will have some regrets, but you will never, ever, regret the time you spent worshipping God and studying His Word.

Questions:

1. Think of specific ways that the "hub" of our lives (Jesus Christ) can affect our everyday activities.

2. List the characteristics mentioned in Hebrews 11. Beside each name, list one action that faith required of him or her.

3. When King Darius made the decree against worshipping God, why didn't Daniel continue to pray in secret? Why do you think he decided to keep praying right in front of his window?

4. What are some times when displaying our faith might be "inconvenient?" During these times, are you under as much pressure as Shadrach, Meshach, and Abednego probably were?

5. Discuss some personal examples of times when something fun or

important was sacrificed in order to worship God. How did that sacrifice affect your faith?

6. Find three verses in Job to which you can refer when you become discouraged. Mark these in your Bible.

7. Find a verse in Hebrews that speaks of faithfulness to the assembly. Mark this verse in your Bible.

Projects

1. Prepare a five minute presentation to present to your study group on your favorite Bible example of faith. Illustrate using power point, posters, or an overhead projector.

2. Teach a preschool Bible class on a character of faith. Have songs and activities prepared.

3. Read the entire book of Job.

4. Be present at every worship assembly and Bible class of your congregation for one entire month.

5. Write three letters to members, preferably in your age group, who need encouragement to attend worship services faithfully.

6. Make a poster-board presentation to your study group illustrating the pie and the wheel comparison. Be sure to include scriptures in the presentation.

CHAPTER THREE:
Unwrap The Present!

Prayer is a beautiful gift we, as Christians, get to open again and again. I am amazed to think that I can instantly stand before God's throne anytime of the day, without having to wait a single moment. God has given us something precious: the opportunity to speak directly to Him whenever, and for however long we want. This chapter will hopefully show you the beauty and necessity of prayer.

The Importance Of Prayer

I once heard of a woman who had all the modern conveniences such as heat, air conditioning, running water, and electricity, but who, for nostalgic reasons, chose not to use any of these "life aids." When asked why, she simply replied, "I want to live exactly the way my grandmother did." So, this determined woman used oil lamps (never flipping a switch), washed her clothes in the river and hung them out to dry, cooked her food over a fire, etc. While I, personally, can't imagine trying to live that way everyday, I guess there is nothing wrong with it. However, it's disturbing to ponder how much simpler this woman's life would be if she'd use what she has and turn on the lights once in a while! It's the same way with prayer. We can have instant light the minute we wish to turn it on, and yet many of us choose to live life the hard way. God will bless us richly if we just talk to him.

James 5:16 reads, "The effectual fervent prayer of a righteous man availeth much." That means we, as Christians, can actually change the mind of God with our prayers! He carefully considers everything we ask, and always gives us what is best for us. James 1:5 reads, "If any of you lack wisdom, let him ask of God that giveth to all men liberally, and upbraideth not, and it shall be given him."

This is one of my favorite Bible verses. Let's break it down into five parts. "If any of you lack wisdom...." God didn't say, "If those who have been Christians a long time lack wisdom...." He didn't say "If any of the elders and deacons lack wisdom...." He said "...**any** of you..." God is willing to give wisdom to ANY Christians who need it! I'd say that would include all Christians...especially me!

"...let him ask of God..." Not ask Dr. Phil or your philosophy teacher. This is heavenly wisdom from the Creator of the universe! "...that giveth to all men liberally..." In other words, God will give us not a little wisdom, but a heaping helping of heavenly wisdom. How refreshing! "...and upbraideth not..." This just means that God is not going to make fun of us in any way. God won't laugh at us when we ask for help. He takes our requests very seriously. "...and it shall be given him." It doesn't say, "...it *may* be given him." It says "...it **shall** be given him." What an awesome promise!

Persistence In Prayer

We've discussed the beauty and importance of prayer, but I suggest to you that if you don't get what you ask for right away, re-examine your motives, making sure they are not selfish, material motives, and remember to ask for what is best.

Luke 11:5-10 tells the story of a man who needed three loaves of bread to give to a friend who was hungry. Verse six indicates that the man had nothing to give to his friend, so he went to a neighbor's house and knocked, asking, "Friend, lend me three loaves, for a friend of mine in his journey is come to me, and I have nothing to set before him." The neighbor replied from behind the door, "Trouble me not; the door is now shut, and my children are with me in bed; I cannot rise and give thee."

The man didn't give up though. He kept knocking until the neighbor got out of bed and helped him. The application of this parable is in verses nine and ten: "Ask, and it shall be given you; seek and ye shall find; knock, and it shall be opened unto you. For everyone that asketh recieveth; and he that seeketh findeth; to him that knocketh it shall be opened."

So the point of the parable is this: Even though you can't always see God's answer to your prayer right away, that doesn't mean you should stop asking. God wants us to be persistent.

Objectives In Prayer

In Matthew 6 we read about what I call the "model prayer." In verses 9-13 Jesus gives us a pattern for prayer. Verse nine reads, "after this manner pray ye." However, this doesn't mean we can't talk to God about anything and in our own words. Jesus was just showing the multitudes what prayer is. Listed here, in Matthew 6 are several requests for spiritual blessings, such as forgiveness, the ability to resist temptation, and help in forgiving others. What I find to be fascinating is that out of all the requests, only one is for something physical; the rest are for spiritual blessings. I think perhaps Jesus was making a point here; we should not focus on physical, material blessings, but, rather, spiritual needs. I also find it interesting that the one physical blessing asked for in Matthew 6 is daily bread, which is needed for survival. Start getting analytical and you'll come to the conclusion that even *this* is a spiritual blessing, because we have to have food so we can live and lead others to Christ.

While it is good to set apart time for prayer everyday, I think it's important that we understand that our line of communication with God is open twenty-four hours. We don't have to make an appointment. There's no waiting in line. I Thessalonians 5:1 reads, "Pray without ceasing." For those of us who aren't clever poets, the word "cease" isn't very prevalent in our everyday vocabulary. In my own words, the verse says, "Pray all of the time." As Christians, we should develop a prayerful spirit. We need to realize that we can talk to God anytime, and about anything.

We don't have to always tell God about some major issue when we pray. It's good to pray about little things, too. We should practice praying short prayers all day long like, "Father, please keep me safe while I drive around today." "Please help me to pass this geography test." "Please give me wisdom and courage as I invite this girl to church." Prayers need to be offered up frequently. God wants us to talk to him all day long. Think about your earthly father. Let's say you set aside five minutes every night to talk to him about what's on your mind, but the rest of the day, you ignore him, and say nothing to him. While he would appreciate the few minutes you save for him each night, he wouldn't consider your relationship a close one.

Practical Suggestions:

Take advantage of time that could be spent in prayer. I often pray while driving alone. If you finish your test early in class, why not spend the rest of the period talking to God? Try spending your time in the shower praying. I always pray at night before I go to sleep. Try to use your time wisely, placing God in a position of high priority in your life (Matthew 6:33).

Make a prayer list or even keep a prayer journal. For most people, it is easier to remember everything that needs to be said if it can be read from a list, instead of just fishing things from memory. Keep a list of all the sick people in your church family, missionaries you know, people who are struggling with sin, and friends who need Christ in their lives. A list can be extremely helpful.

Tell people frequently that you will pray for them, and always keep your promises. It means the world to me when I know someone who loves me is taking my name before the throne of God. Make it a habit to do this for others.

So, go ahead, open the present! If you're a Christian, it has your name on it. Don't ever take this treasure for granted.

Questions:

1. Find three prayers of the Old Testament. Were the prayers answered? Is the God of the New Covenant the same Jehovah? Is He any less powerful?

2. List the five things requested in the model prayer of Matthew 6. Which is a "physical" request?

3. Give some Biblical examples of people who had strong relationships with God because of their constant, prayerful spirits.

4. What are some spiritual blessings for which we, as Christians, should ask?

5. What are some examples of time during your day that could be spent in prayer?

6. What are some things we should always remember in prayer (examples: political leaders, sick people, etc.)?

Projects

1. Make a prayer list. Divide your list into categories such as your physical needs, the physical needs of others, prayer for lost souls, prayer for our nation, your spiritual needs, the leaders of your congregation, etc. Pray with your list in hand and in mind every day for an entire month.

2. Set aside a specific fifteen minute period (example: 6:30 a.m. to 6:45 a.m.) that you will spend in prayer everyday for a week. Choose a new time and place for prayer. Every time you are in this place, be praying. Do this for two weeks (examples: while you're driving alone, in the shower, or perhaps between classes at school).

3. Ask five mentors to pray for your spiritual needs. Write each of these
   a note of thanks for helping you grow as a Christian.
4. Tell at least ten people (some of which should be non-Christians) that
   you are praying for them. Do this in one week.

CHAPTER FOUR:
Who's In Charge?!

Respect for authority is a God-given command, but that doesn't mean it is an easy task in our time. The societal revolution of the 1960s gave Americans a whole new perspective on individuality, personal feelings, and self-gratification. It brought on the widespread opinion that respect for any one or any thing, save yourself, is a sign of weakness. Society scoffs at wives submitting to husbands, church members obeying elders, and children honoring parents.

I was waiting to be seated at Chili's the other day, and it didn't take me long to notice a little boy, seven or eight years old, standing in front of me. Because of the crowd, we were squeezed into a small foyer right outside the dining hall. It was tight with people, and this little boy was not helping any. He stood in front of the doors with his arms outspread, and yelled at random people who had been called to be seated. He kept shouting, "What's the secret password?" The little boy refused to step aside and continued to badger the would-be customers. What was worse was that the man who was supposedly in charge of the boy just stood there and rolled his eyes. When his girlfriend, the mother of the child, returned from her cigarette break outside, the man told her what her son had been doing, and she simply stood there and laughed at the boy! For Pete's sake, had I behaved like him when I was his age, I would have been *worn out*. But this is just an example of what you and I see every day. It's the kids who are in charge. Parents often seem to have given up on the whole respect thing.

As I get older, I am becoming increasingly disgusted with teenagers' attitudes toward elderly people. They act as if old people are just here on earth to be ridiculed. This is often a problem even within the church. While there are countless advantages of being part of an active youth group, many times the members of that group tend to seclude themselves from the rest of the congregation. It's almost like a separate congregation in the same building. Such teens are missing out on so much by not engaging in fellowship with all ages, not just their own.

Teens seem to be terrified by the thought that they could have a conversation with an elderly person, and enjoy it. It's just not cool to do that. Hugs, cards, and visits into the homes of those people are out of the question. It's not unusual for me to see teens walk inside a restaurant or store, letting the door slam in the faces of slow-moving elderly people. Elevators are often filled by young people who rush in front of old people who can't make it there as quickly. Common courtesy seems to be a thing of the past.

Another example of disrespect is outright disobedience. I don't need to spell this one out. Mom says you're grounded and you can't get on the internet, but you do it anyway after she goes to bed.

So, why is the problem of disrespect so prevalent in America today? I've thought of a list of reasons. While you read on, do some of your own brainstorming and think of more reasons why respectful teens are few and far between.

Lack Of Belief In God

Over time Americans have become more and more skeptical about the existence of a higher being that created this earth. This is the chief reason for disrespect. If there is no supreme authority watching what we say and do, then why should we try to please anyone but ourselves? There is no motivation if there is no God.

Lack Of Respect For Religion

During a recent discussion with my mother I learned that in the 1950s, practically everyone attended church services somewhere every Sunday. Times have changed. In some cases, people have become workaholics in the true sense of the word, losing all sense of reverence for the Lord's church and worship. In other cases, Sundays are reserved for activities such as shopping, fishing, homework, or perhaps just catching up on sleep. When parents give their kids the idea that worshiping God is not important, those children automatically decide that God's rules for behavior must not be important either. In so deciding, they lose regard for codes of morality and those who would enforce those codes.

Feminism

When women decided that they belonged in the workplace rather than in the home with their families, children sustained a great loss. In my opinion, mothers are the primary reason anyone learns to respect authority. Instead of one standard set in the home, many children have been under many authorities; babysitters, grandmothers, day-care workers, etc. It's no wonder children don't learn to respect authority. They have so many different authorities at such young ages that they don't know what real authority is. In their innocent confusion, they give up on respect altogether.

No One Accepts Responsibility For Discipline

Many times parents tend to shift their jobs of raising children to someone else; the school system, the youth minister, or perhaps the Christian college. What's everyone's job tends to be nobody's job. Parents need to take charge of their children, instead of ignoring them and expecting someone else to instill humility and respect in their hearts.

The "Victim Mentality"

"It's not my fault because my parents were poor."
"It's not my fault because my father abused me."

"It's not my fault because my mom did drugs."

Does this sound familiar? Probably. We live in a "poor me" society. It's everywhere.

It's in our legal system. Criminals are getting by with light sentences because of their terrible home lives during the formative years; or maybe they're just sent somewhere for therapy. Capitol punishment is all but a thing of the past.

It's in our school system. Students are not expected to perform well and make good grades because they have learning disabilities. While learning disabilities can be real obstacles to success, many times the term "Learning Disability" is not clearly defined and may be too frequently applied. Some so-called "experts" even estimate that 20% of American children may be learning disabled. This scenario results in a weakening of standards of excellence or standards of authority. Additionally, people blame the government when their kids are making poor grades, saying, "The school system has not been allocated enough money. That's why my kids aren't getting the education they need." It's been proven time and again that children can soar academically when guided by loving and supportive parents and teachers. Money is secondary to moral and academic standards in achieving goals of education.

It's in the workplace. Employers are required to hire a certain percentage of minority workers. Thus, qualifications and a healthy work ethic often become secondary to ethnicity. Because of this mentality, standards are lowered and systems of authority become ineffective.

Now that we've acknowledged there's a problem of disrespect in our society and addressed why it's there, let's ask ourselves what we, as teens, can do personally to change this environment of disregard for figures of authority. I've thought of some practical ways, but you can think of some of your own.

Parents

How serious is God about respecting our parents? As young people still living at home, we are commanded by Him to honor them. We are New Testament Christians, and we are no longer under the rules of the

Old Testament. However, we can learn so much about our Creator by studying them. The Old Testament is exceedingly clear in reference to respect; it's like looking right into the heart of God.

II Kings 2:23-24 tells the story of some little children who made fun of Elisha's bald head. Elisha turned around and cursed them in the name of the Lord. Immediately following, two bears came out of the woods and devoured forty-two children. Evidently, God was not pleased with this display of disrespect on the part of these kids!

Deuteronomy 21:18-21 commanded all parents living in the Mosaic age to have their sons publicly stoned if they were "stubborn and rebellious." Does that sound like any of your friends? Stubborn and rebellious? Had they been born during this time they would have been publicly humiliated and stoned immediately because of their disregard for authority.

Deuteronomy 5:16 says, "Honor thy father and thy mother as the Lord thy God has commanded thee; that thy days may be prolonged, and that it may go well with thee."

When someone says we should respect figures of authority, we tend to instantly picture police officers or the school principal, but God forthrightly teaches that we should respect and honor our parents. Talk about denying culture! Lucky for us, God doesn't handle disrespect the way he did with the bears or the stoning anymore. We must keep in mind that while we may not be stricken dead the minute we smart off to Mom or Dad, God will have no patience for disrespectful teens on the Judgment Day.

While the Old Testament is clear about God's demand for respecting our parents, the New Testament is equally clear. Ephesians 6:1-3 reads, "Children, obey your parents in the Lord; for this is right. Honor thy father and mother; which is the first commandment with promise; that it may be well with thee, and thou mayest live long upon the earth." As in Deuteronomy, God promises good things to those who honor their parents in this passage. Verse 3 basically says, "Be respectful, and you'll find happiness." It also says that this is not just a request. It's a command. God is serious!

So what are some practical ways that we can show honor and gratitude to our parents? There are lots of things we can do, but in my mind, it's easier to understand the things I *shouldn't* do instead of the things I *should* do. Here is a list of some "don'ts," but you think of some of your own:

*Don't roll your eyes when your parents are talking to you. This is especially difficult for me because I don't always know when I'm doing it. What I do know is this: eye rolling is a known sign of disrespect; therefore we need to refrain from it.

*Don't smart off. I've always thought that there is a respectful way to state your opinion about something, but there is also a disrespectful way. Stay calm. Never yell. Try not to interrupt them when they are scolding you. Wait until there is a pause to speak. Never use sarcasm to illustrate your point. Remember, we don't always have to agree with them, but we ALWAYS have to respect them.

*Don't manipulate them. Don't try to do things behind their backs. Just obey them in everything. I know this is so much easier said than done, but, in choosing to deliberately disobey them, whether they know about it or not, you will damn your soul if you don't repent (I didn't say that—God did!).

*Don't raise your voice to them, stomp away, or slam doors when you disagree with them.

*Don't walk away while they are speaking to you.

Elderly People

They're people too, you know. Many old folks are lonely, and love to see young people who are interested in their happiness and well-being. Show them you care! Here are a few suggestions of ways to do that:

*Write little notes of encouragement. These don't have to be long and time-consuming. Just a little note to say, "I'm thinking about you."

*Hug! I don't think there is anything old people like more than warm hugs from kids like us.

*Perform little acts of courtesy. Always open doors for elderly folks making their way toward a door. Help them carry groceries to their cars or lend a hand wherever they may need you.

*Let them talk. Old people love to talk. Go visit some folks in a nursing home and you'll see what I mean. Many of them simply need someone to sit in front of them, nod, and laugh occasionally, to be happy. Give them this privilege. Just let them chatter. The main thing is, be interested! Put on your excited face and give them the joy of telling you about the good ole' days.

School

Present an attitude of humility toward your school authorities. Give your teachers the respect they deserve. Listen in class. Study hard to make good grades. Don't ever say "yeah." Say "yes ma'am" or "yes sir." Show them that you want to honor them for the time they're sacrificing to give you a proper education.

At The Workplace

At the time this chapter was written, I was working at a fast food restaurant. I was amazed daily at the attitudes of some of the employees toward the manager. One of my co-workers, "Misty", was constantly smarting off to our employer, rolling her eyes, and saying "Whatever," when he criticized her. Don't expect to get a raise if you don't honor your boss with your words and attitude, but most importantly, don't expect to be pleasing to God when you dishonor those above you in the workplace!

With The Law (Romans 13:1)

This is simple enough. Don't do things that you know are illegal, unless you must in order to obey the laws we read in the New Testament. Law enforcers are not there to make us miserable; they're there to serve and protect us (Romans 13:3). Don't speak disrespectfully about the police or the law itself.

With The General Public

Everyone deserves some bit of respect--even strangers.

*Look people in the eyes when you speak to them.

*Give a firm handshake.

*Be considerate! Open doors! Say "Please" and "Thank you!" Use the manners you heard about in preschool. You might be the first friendly, smiling face someone has seen all day. Show people that Christians are happy people!

As I mentioned at the beginning of this chapter, respect is no easy task. It takes a lot of will power, self-control, and usually a lot of prayer. Many people say, Oh, I respect God, of course! But let me remind you: If you don't respect the authorities I've discussed in this chapter, you don't truly respect God (Romans 13:2).

May the Lord bless you as you strive to display the honor and awe you feel for Him in simple, everyday ways.

Questions:

1. Discuss ways that you can become actively involved in the lives of church
   members which are outside your youth group.

2. Think of some "do's" in reference to how you treat your parents.

3. List some examples of societal disrespect you've seen during the past week.

4. Give an example from your experience of someone who has the "victim mentality." Is this mode of thinking productive? Do you know someone else who truly is a victim of some disease of circumstance, but maintains an "I can do it" attitude? Which person is more respectful of authority?

5. Do you think Jesus was respectful of his parents? Cite a passage about his parental respect.

6. Do you think appearance (clothing, grooming, facial expressions) can convey respect or disrespect in certain situations? Discuss.

Projects

1. Keep a list of every disrespectful occurrence or scenario that you see in one day. Bring your list to your study group for discussion.

2. Write a 300-word essay on the negative effects of the feminist movement in America. Bring the essay to your study group for discussion.

3. For one week, clip every article from your city's newspaper that illustrates the problem of disrespect in society. Highlight pertinent facts. Assemble clippings in a booklet. Bring to your study group.

4. Do a study about capitol punishment. Is it Biblical? Present a five-minute defense of your opinion for your study group.

5. Get a good concordance. Read every verse that contains the word "respect." Make a list of those that are commanding respect. Who should be respected from these verses?

6. Choose five people whose authority you should respect. Write each a letter expressing your gratitude and honor.

7. Write a letter to your parents expressing gratitude and pledging your honor to them. Mail the letter.

8. Visit a nursing home once a week for a month. Prepare a card or small gift and present it to a resident at each visit.

9. Organize a youth trip to a nursing home to sing hymns for the residents. Arrange a time for this activity with the social worker at the home.

Works Cited

William J. Bennett, Chester E. Finn, Jr. and John T. E. Cribb, Jr., The Educated Child, (New York: The Free Press, 1999), p. 471

CHAPTER FIVE:
Sticks and Stones

One of the most powerful tools we, as women, use is verbal communication. Are you aware that women speak, on the average, about 30% to 50% more words than men do each day? That means, as girls, we can do 30% to 50% more good OR 30% to 50% more evil than our male counterparts. Just think about that! What you are inside comes out of you when you talk. People judge you by the words you say (Matthew 12:34, Luke 6:45). Choosing the right words for each conversation is a vital task. This chapter will include some practical ways we, as Christian girls, can find ways to use our mouths to please God. Remember these pointers as you strive to use your words as a means of edification, rather than destruction.

Is It Dirty?

What are dirty words? 1 Thessalonians 2:3,4 reads, "For our exhortation was not of deceit nor of uncleanness, nor in guile: But as we were allowed of God to be put in trust with the gospel, even so we speak; not as pleasing men, but God, which trieth our hearts."

I looked up the word "unclean" (or dirty as we would say) in

Thayer's Greek-English Lexicon of the New Testament. The first definition was in reference to our bodies being dirty, but the second definition is as follows, "...In a moral sense, the impurity of lustful, luxurious, profligate living."

According to Paul in this verse, the words people speak can reflect a "lustful, luxurious, profligate" lifestyle.

When writing this chapter, I struggled with the decision of whether I should travel, word by word, through the enormous world of foul language. I decided that most girls reading this book already know just about every repugnant word our modern peers use, whether you learned them at school, at work, at play rehearsal, or perhaps even among your youth group (I hope not!!).

Many words that provoke impure and usually sexual visions in our minds are frequently thrown around in our world like leaves on a windy autumn day. We can hardly escape hearing vulgarities about various parts of the human body, about sexuality, or about obscene subjects. You know. You hear these words. There are many words that are recognized as dirty words, but there are also some that are considered "mild" in our culture. I said I wasn't going to define specific words for you, but I feel it is necessary for me to tell you about one phrase which seems to fool everyone, even those who are Christians. Perhaps most people don't know what it means. It's a phrase we all hear constantly. You may have said it lately without any tinge of guilt. It's the phrase that usually goes, this or that "sucks." You may be rolling your eyes, but before you call me radical, please read what it means. The definition of our word "sucks" used as a slang term means "engages in fellatio (oral sex)." As I am writing this, I am blushing with embarrassment, but I feel that you should know the true meaning of this word that has become so socially acceptable. I certainly can't see the logic behind a Christian using this word after reading Philippians 4:8 which says, "Finally, brethren, whatsoever things are true, whatsoever things are honest, whatsoever things are just, whatsoever things are pure, whatsoever things are lovely, whatsoever things are of good report; if there be any virtue, and if there be any praise, think on these things."

Does such a word fit into any of those categories? The answer is obvious. Not only do I want to encourage you to keep your mouth clean of foul language, but I also pray that God will give you enough courage to say something when you hear those around you use such speech. Stand up for what you believe. Chances are your friends will respect you for it. Practice asking politely that they not use those words in your presence. When my friends ask me why, I simply tell them that hearing them use profanity makes it difficult for me to keep my own words and thoughts pure. If you are kind and gentle in your request, they will probably make the effort to accommodate your wishes. If not, they don't respect you and they are probably not the type of people you need to hang around.

Is It Disrespectful?

Many words and phrases that blaspheme my Lord have become commonplace. Most people just don't think about the meaning of these words.

When your friends say "oh my god," they probably aren't talking about God at all. They are using His holy name merely as an interjection; an expression of surprise or shock. You may hear, "oh my gosh," "lord, yes," or "lord, no," "jeez." "golly" or "gee." Or maybe, your friends just type "OMG" on your Facebook wall. All of these are euphemisms for the Lord's name. They are not used to reverence God at all. One of the Ten Commandments in Exodus 20:7 is, "Thou shalt not take the name of the Lord, thy God, in vain. For the Lord will not hold him guiltless who takes His name in vain."

That just means that we're not to use His name lightly, but with reverence. One chilling thought indicated in the words, "...the Lord shall not hold him guiltless..." is that when I use his name in vain, I am guilty before God.

Other words we call curse words are more easily recognized. The word "damn" is short for "damnation," so when you hear someone say, "damn this or that," she is condemning that person or object to hell. The words "darn," and "dang" are euphemisms for the word "damn."

I am disgusted when I hear people put the words "God" and "damn" together. When some people get especially angry or irritated, they may say "Goddamn it!" I often want to say, "Do you realize that you just put the holy name of the eternal One who wants to save you in front of a blasphemous curse?"

The word "hell" is often used lightly, as well. We hear the phrases "oh, what the hell?" or "the hell with it", or sometimes "hell, no" or "hell, yes." Hell is not something to joke about, people! It is a real place filled with real anguish and ultimate punishment and the word "hell" should not be used casually. The word "heck" is a "softer version" of "hell."

Let us be sure that the words we use are reflecting the respect we have toward our Creator.

Is It Destructive?

Studies have always shown that boys tend to release anger or jealousy inside of them by some physical act (like giving their enemies a knuckle sandwich), while a girl's greatest weapon is her tongue. For example, if Bill stole Jim's girlfriend, Jim might walk up to Bill when he sees him and punch him in the nose.

Let's look at a different scenario, this time using girls:

Pam has had a crush on Henry since sixth grade. Henry never asked her out, but she always knew he had a thing for her. They would pass notes in class and sit together during lunch. One day a pretty girl named Jan moved to town and within one week, Henry asked Jan out on a date. Instead of walking up to Jan and slapping her, Pam began talking about Jan to all her classmates, making up stories which put Jan in a very negative light, or embellishing true stories to make Jan look bad.

You know what I'm talking about. This is what girls do. We tend to use words as tools to push someone else down while elevating ourselves. Before you say something about someone else, be sure you ask yourself why you're saying it. Will saying this help the person I'm talking about or will it hurt that person? Always consider whether you would want the same things said about you. If not, don't say it (Matthew 7:12). That applies to what you listen to, as well. If your friends are trash-talking someone you know, ask them to stop or simply leave the room. Rather than to break others down with your tongue, use your tongue to build others up by your kindness. Strike up a conversation with someone who is sitting alone. Don't let yourself be a part of any clique. Don't let anyone feel unwanted or out of place. New studies show that the part of your brain that registers pain reacts the exact same way when you feel socially rejected as when you've been poked in the eye. In other words, it's been proven that it hurts us to be an outcast!

Don't Gossip

It only hurts others, and will eventually hurt you. Include everyone in conversations and treat everyone with kindness. I know this is hard, especially if there is someone you "just can't stand." God tells us in Romans 12: 20, 21: "Therefore if thine enemy hunger, feed him; if he thirst, give him drink; for in so doing thou shalt heap coals of fire on his head. Be not overcome with evil, but overcome evil with good."

That means that if you really want to get back, show your enemy kindness. She probably won't know quite how to respond. It's possible that she might respond with returned kindness. Let God handle the vengeance.

Compliments are almost vital in the life of a teenage girl. Use your tongue to compliment another, whether it is about something she said, how she did in a ballgame, her performance in a play, or simply her appearance. Some people will respect you instantly if you just encourage them with your words. This is especially true about girls who are younger than you. I remember the thrill I experienced as a little girl when a teenager would say something nice to me. I would think about it for days. Little girls want to be just like you. Show them the kindness of a Christian. I suggest you sometimes send them little notes of encouragement, or ask them to sit with you in worship. If you are a teenage girl, little girls sometimes look to you as their role models more than they do their own parents, whether the parents like it or not. We must take on that grave responsibility and be someone that's okay to emulate.

Try To Avoid:

"She thinks she's so cool."
"Look at those shoes. They must be her mom's."
"She's such a flirt!"

"She's the only one that just doesn't get it."
"Does it look like I care?"
"She's such a dork."

Instead Try:

"She impresses me. She's got a great attitude!"
"I'm really proud of the way you stood up for what was right."
"I'm here for you if you need me."
"I just want you to know that I'm praying for you."
"You really encourage me!"

Is It Deceptive?

Speech that deceives is also condemned in scripture. The Bible is so clear when it comes to lying. In Revelation 21:8 God says, "...all liars shall have their part in the lake which burneth with fire and brimstone: which is the second death."

There are lots of ways we may deceive with our words. Here are a few:

An outright lie: This is the obvious lie. If your little sister got ketchup all over your history report and, upon your asking, said she didn't do it, that's an outright lie.

A "technical" truth: Have you ever said, "Well, technically I was telling the truth"? As an example, let's say you answer the phone, and the person on the other line says he wants to talk to your sister. You know it's someone your sister doesn't want to talk to, so you do your sister a favor and push her out the back door, and reply, "Sorry, she's out." Technically, that's the truth, but the deceit, the essence of what you said, is a lie.

False flattery: Even if you mean well, lying to make someone else feel good is wrong. Perhaps you have a good friend who didn't like the way she looked, so she dyed her black hair blonde and got a perm, and it looks so bad. You know she has low self-esteem as it is, so when she asks, you just say, "Yeah, it looks cool!" You know it would hurt her feelings if you tell her what you really think, so you just tell a little lie.

That would be false flattery.

Assent to someone else's lie: Imagine that you're going to spend the evening with your best friend, even though you both have to take the ACT the next morning. Before coming to pick you up, your friend told her mom that the two of you were going to study together, so her mom said okay. Instead of studying, you meet your boyfriends at the movies. When you get back to your friend's house to spend the night, your friend's mom says, "Did you go to the library to study?" Your friend says, "Yeah." Then her mom looks at you and says, "Did you have fun?" to which you reply, "Yeah, I did." You had fun, but not doing what your friend said you did.

We've all heard that a lie just gets bigger and bigger because when we tell one, we have to tell another to cover for the first one. There is no form of lying that is okay. Little white lies will damn us just the same as big black ones. I would much rather face the consequences of telling the truth now than to spend an eternity burning in hell.

If your answer to any of these questions is "yes" in reference to your own speech, I pray that you will seek the bountiful forgiveness that God is willing to give us, and the forgiveness of those to whom or about whom you have spoken wrongly.

One last thought: Matthew 12:36 says, "But I say to you that for every idle word men may speak, they will give account of it in the day of judgment." Do the right thing. Think before you speak.

Questions:

1. Can you find other verses that are about keeping your heart and speech pure?

2. What are some other euphemisms to avoid that are not mentioned in this chapter?

3. Find at least two scriptures that show what God thinks about gossip.

4. Why do people gossip? Are there any good reasons to gossip?

5. To whom does vengeance belong (Romans 12)?

6. Have you ever asked your friends to stop talking in a vulgar or disrespectful way? What was their reaction? Did they respect you for it?

7. Think of some additional ways we can build others up with our words. Practice these in class.

Projects:

1. Find ten Bible passages that instruct us about purity of thoughts and speech. Write them clearly on index cards and post them around your bedroom and bathroom. Leave these up for at least one month. Give another set of the same verses on index cards to a friend, so she can do the same if she wishes.

2. Make a list of the ten most common curses and/or ways you hear God's name taken in vain in your daily life. Carry this index card with you, and put a mark beside the phrases you hear, each time you hear them. At the end of the week,   study the list you've made. What word or phrase did you hear most often? Can you recall certain situations or people that caused a lot of marks? Are there any situations that you can avoid to keep from hearing the profanity as much?

3. Send five encouraging notes to five different younger girls during each week this month. Include praise for positive attributes and a verse of scripture in each.

4. Ask a younger girl, or a group of younger girls to sit with you during each
    service during the next month.

5. Take a stack of index cards, a marker, and a role of double stick tape to school with you one day. Encourage at least twelve people by

placing encouraging "way-to-go-notes" on their lockers, desks, text books, etc. Include scripture when appropriate.

6. Find five instances in scripture when lying or deception led to more sin. Bring your list and Bible references to the next study sessions and discuss with mentor.

7. Write a children's fable or fairy story about someone who gets in big trouble because of a lie. Ask one of the young children's teachers in your congregation if you can visit a children's class and read your story. Be sure to apply the story to the children's lives when you finish reading.

8. Check the newspaper every day for a month for current events or court cases that include deception. Compile these in a folder or scrapbook and turn them in to your mentor at the next meeting.

9. Write an essay on a famous historical character whose legacy was marred by deception. Read this aloud at the next meeting. List and define the sins listed in Revelation 21:8. Discuss in a study session how that all liars will share eternity with those who have committed these sins.

Works Cited

Most of the material in this chapter was taken from Hannah Colley. "Speech" in Girl to Girl. Ed. Laura Elliott. Huntsville, AL, Publishing Designs, 2005

Paul Recer, "Pain of social rejection as great as poke in eye," 2003, Huntsville (AL) Times, P. A1 and A6.

CHAPTER SIX:
Fashion Tips 101
What NOT to Wear

"How do I look?" Those four little words have always been at the top of our lists of overused vocabulary as teenage girls. Admit it. Most of us girls love to look pretty! That's why we always have to try everything on before we buy it, unlike some of our guy friends, who refuse to spend more than five minutes in a clothing store. We have to make sure an outfit is flattering before we spend our money on it. What we need to work on is not just asking ourselves "is this pretty?" but "is this modest?"

This is not something that's easy for me to write about. This is mainly because I'm a girl, and I can't understand the temptation guys deal with in reference to visual stimulation. The following comments are taken from a survey of teenage guys, ages fourteen to twenty-four who were asked questions about the way girls dress:

It is important that you realize there are young men struggling in ways you can't understand.

I do not think that most girls understand the thoughts that go through men's heads when they see a girl dressing the way she shouldn't—or she definitely wouldn't dress that way.

Boys certainly view what girls wear differently than girls view what other girls wear.

Guys are weak in this area. Immodest dress doesn't help us out.

I would love to tell all Christian girls that they have an enormous power and influence over Christian men simply by the way they dress.

I do not believe the average girl understands how much of a problem lust causes for the average guy. For the most part, the lust is visual.

Whether they realize it or not, girls are a part of this problem. A true Christian sister would consider how her dress will affect her Christian brothers.

And one of my personal favorites...

"Dress modestly. We dig it."

Guys are obviously wired differently than we are. Reading these quotes really makes me want to do whatever I can to help my Christian brothers fight the temptation of lust. I can't stand the thought that when I don't dress modestly, Satan is using me to tempt God's people. A lot of girls think that it's just a lost cause; there's nothing you can do to keep men from thinking sexual thoughts about girls. God tells us something different, and that's why I'm writing this chapter. No immodestly dressed girl can force a guy to lust. Men have a choice. However, as our clothing gets tighter and more revealing, it becomes much easier for the guys around us to sin. We girls have to realize that there is something we can do to help our Christian brothers in their walk with God.

Why Should I Be Modest?

I Timothy 2:9, 10 reads, "In like manner also, that women adorn themselves in modest apparel, with shamefacedness and sobriety, not with braided hair or gold, or pearls, or costly array; But that which becometh women professing godliness with good works." Okay, so we know from reading this verse that God wants us to dress modestly. Now read Matthew 5:28.

"But I say unto you, that whosoever looketh on a woman to lust after her hath committed adultery with her already in his heart."

So, obviously, men can simply look at us and sin. As scary as it is, we have the ability to become an enormous stumbling block for our brothers. God desires that we avoid this (Romans 14:13, Matthew 18:7).

While the Bible is clear about God's desire for us to dress modestly, and that should be enough to motivate us to do so, I've noticed that girls who don't flaunt themselves get a lot more respect from the guys. The Christian guys quoted previously were asked what a girl's dress reveals about her character.

Here are some of the answers they gave:

It reveals how seriously she takes herself, her Christianity, and any relationships she might be in.

What her priorities are; what kind of beauty she values.

What she wants to be noticed for.

Whether she is boastful or humble.

What she wants guys to think about when looking at her.

How much she respects herself; how much she wants to be respected.

How she expects to be treated.

Whether or not she carefully considers and applies the practical implications of God's word.

Girls who show a lot of skin are usually trashy.

Girls who wear immodest clothes will not appear to be Christians.

I believe a girl who takes the time to find modest clothes and so dress in a way that is not a stumbling block professes true godliness.

We learn from passages such as I Peter 2:11 that God wants us to avoid sexual lust at all costs. Of course girls struggle with lust sometimes, but most of the time, it's much more difficult for guys than it is for us. If we love our brothers with agape love, we will dress for their spiritual benefit rather than for our comfort or to suit our preferences.

In a class of Christian senior high guys who attended a leadership workshop recently, this question was asked: "What is your greatest obstacle in trying to be what God wants you to be while you are here this week?" The unanimous answer was, "It's the way the girls dress." Christian girls should never place obstacles in the spiritual paths of our brothers. Agape love demands that we unselfishly do whatever it takes to help bear each other's burdens.

We realize now that in order to help guys out, we have to dress modestly. Great. But what does that mean?

What Kind Of Clothing Is Not Modest?

The surveyed Christian guys were asked to specifically share what kind of clothing they thought was immodest. They unanimously agreed that low-cut shirts and thin, "see-through" garments (without additional clothing underneath) are undoubtedly immodest. Sixty-five percent said that shirts that reveal a girl's lower back when she sits down or bends over are immodest. Over 75% agreed that tight shirts are immodest. The majority said tight jeans are immodest. Nearly half said that skirts and shorts above the knee are immodest.

Almost all of the guys surveyed said that sleeveless shirts are modest, but several elaborated to say that "spaghetti strap" shirts and tank tops are immodest.

What about swimsuits? I think many girls who otherwise dress modestly fail to apply standards of modesty when it comes to swimwear. Many people seem to think that going to the beach gives you a license to take off your clothes. I know this is hard to accept, but girls, let's be honest with ourselves. If a guy struggles with lust when we wear tight jeans or low-cut shirts, what makes you think he doesn't lust when we wear something skin-tight that reveals all of our legs, most of our backs, and part of our chests? I mentioned I Timothy 2:9, 10 earlier, which tells us that God wants us to dress in modest apparel. Notice that God's not telling us to dress. He's telling us how to dress. We see here that some forms of apparel (clothing) are modest. Hence, there are obviously some kinds of clothing that are not modest. If swimwear doesn't fall into that category, I honestly don't know what does.

I was recently hanging out with a Christian guy and we were walking through the park on a lovely spring day. We were walking in one direction when he suddenly stopped and said, "Let's turn around and go the other way." When I asked him why, he said, "Did you not see all those girls laying out over there? I try to stay away from places where girls are dressed like that, because it causes a lot of temptation." This was enough for me to know that we are certainly not helping guys out when we go out in a swimsuit!

What Can I Do?

Now that we've addressed why I should be modest and what specifically is not modest, let's talk about what we can do about it. As a teenage girl, I completely understand that it's really hard for us to always know if what we're wearing is modest. One thing that helps me personally is to walk down what I call the "Daddy Runway." When I'm unsure about an outfit, I let my dad take a look before I leave the house. He usually makes this signal with his forefinger which means, "turn around," and I turn around. This is pretty routine at my house. It may sound silly, but my Dad knows exactly what's too tight or too revealing and I know he'll give me an honest answer coming from a heart inhabited by Christ. I shared this with a girls' class when I was in San Andres, Colombia on a mission trip, and one girl in the class raised her hand and said, "What if your dad isn't a Christian, and he doesn't really care about what guys think about you?" This question broke my heart and caused me to thank God for the father I have, and to consider what a girl in her shoes could do to be absolutely sure of her purity in reference to dress. Here's what I came up with: Before you leave the house, look in the mirror and pretend you're about to spend the day with Jesus himself. How would He view what you're wearing? If the thought makes you uncomfortable, you'd better change your outfit, because Jesus IS with you everywhere you go. When in doubt, DON'T!

We need to realize that guys worth waiting for are ones who value what we are on the inside much more than what we are on the outside. One of my favorite passages is I Peter 3:3, 4 which reads, "Whose adorning let it not be that outward adorning of plaiting the hair, and of wearing of gold, or of putting on apparel; But let it be the hidden man of the heart, in that which is not corruptible, even the ornament of a meek and quiet spirit, which is in the sight of God of great price." Yes, it's fun to look pretty, but it's not important. God sees the heart.

Some more quotes from the guys:

It is very true that guys are concerned with physical attraction to a girl—how she looks. But any girl can attract guys' attention when she is wearing immodest clothing. A truly beautiful girl, however, is one who is beautiful inside and out—and she shows this by wearing modest clothing.

Dress is the first thing I notice about a girl. If she is wearing something too low or too tight…I'm not interested!

There is nothing better than a girl who dresses modestly. Guys are attracted to her and not "those."

Coming from a Christian guy, if you want to be attractive, try revealing the hidden person of the heart which has the imperishable quality of a gentle and quiet spirit. To me, that is attractive.

If you're looking for a guy with a heart like these guys have, you will attract him with your purity, rather than impress him with your sexy outfit. If you want a guy to really respect you, respect yourself by dressing modestly. I think many girls wear revealing things to make up for their lack of self-confidence.

I know what I've said in this chapter is not popular, and it's not easy to apply to your personal life. Please understand that it isn't me saying it--it's my heavenly Father, and this is what He wants for us.

May God bless you as you strive to please Him in the way that you dress.

Questions:

1. Find other Bible passages which address the sin of lust or passages about focusing on the heart rather than the body.

2. Discuss current fashions and, through your discussion, determine whether or not those fashions are modest. Discuss ways that we can make something that is fashionable modest (example: try wearing a tank-top underneath a trendy low-cut shirt to make it cover your chest).

3. Find several translations of the word "shamefacedness" (mentioned in I Timothy 2:9, 10). How should this word affect the way I dress?

4. Look up the Greek definitions of the word "lasciviousness" (mentioned in Galatians 5:19-21). Can these definitions have anything to do with the way I dress?

5. Are there any activities at school that we should avoid because of the issue of modesty? Discuss.

Projects:

1. Organize a fashion show! The girls in your group will be the participants and the show will occur at the next meeting. You will need half of the outfits to be modest and half to be immodest. Rotate between modest and immodest. Give excuses people use and scriptural answers to those excuses. (Example: A girl walks out in a mini skirt and says, "It's not my fault if a guy lusts when he looks at me." Next, a modestly dressed girl walks out and reads I Timothy 2:9, 10.) Make sure there are no guys present for this event! ☺

2. Organize a teen girls "purity day" or a special class on modesty for the girls of your congregation and their friends. Invite a faithful woman of your congregation to teach on the importance of modesty.

3. Read *Christian Modesty and The Public Undressing of America* by Jeff Pollard. Although this book was not written by a New Testament Christian, it provides many insightful statistics and opinions on the issue of modesty. After reading the   book, write a book report on it and prepare to present your report at the next meeting. If you are unable to find this book at your local library, you may order it from The Vision Forum, Inc. by calling 800-440-0022.

4. Read the tract, *Why I quit going to the beach* by Tracy L. Moore and write a report on the booklet. Prepare to present your report at the next meeting. The tract can be ordered online at housetohouse.com. You may also access the booklet by contacting Allen Webster by writing him at 329 Nesbit Street NW, Jacksonville, AL, 36265 or by calling him at (256)435-9356.

5. Create a similar survey to the one quoted in this chapter, and get the opinions of the Christian guys in your congregation. You may want to pass it on to Christian guys in surrounding churches, as well. Discuss your results at the next meeting.

6. Buy a fashion catalog or magazine which features today's upcoming fashions and, at your next meeting, discuss whether they are conducive to your modesty standards.

Works Cited

Survey on modesty taken from Allison Boyd. *"Exclusive! What Guys Really Want (Dressing Purely)."* In Girl To Girl. Ed. Laura Elliott. Huntsville, AL, Publishing Designs, 2005

CHAPTER SEVEN:
The Right Moves

Dance...something the whole world glorifies. Danny Kaye sang, *"The best things happen when you're dancing"* in the enchanting musical, *White Christmas*. Garth Brooks admits he preferred to have his heart broken rather than to miss that one dance, in his old song, *"The Dance."* Whitney Houston belted it out in her song, *"I Wanna Dance With Somebody."* Fred Astaire once sang, *"You can take my breakfast, you can take my lunch, you can take my women, but if swing goes, I go too."* It's just a wholesome activity for everyone...or is it? Consider this chapter your personal "dancing lesson." Then you can decide for yourself whether or not dancing is for you.

What Is Dancing?

Dictionary.com defines it as follows: "To move rhythmically, usually to music, using prescribed or improvised steps and gestures." Dancing can be a party activity, a hobby, or a sport. It can be done alone, with one person of the opposite sex, or sometimes with several people. It always involves some sort of movement of the body. People of all ages are involved in dancing. So, what's the big deal? How can something so widely accepted be wrong? I admit I have struggled with this question. There are some forms of dancing in our world that are pure, clean fun. We know this not only by using our common sense, but also by reading biblical examples. In Exodus 15:20-21, Miriam led a group of women in a dance and song praising God for delivering them safely through the dangers of the Red Sea. Was her dancing promoting or endorsing sin in any form? Of course not. She may have been moving her body in some jubilant motion because of the awe and admiration she was feeling, but there is no way we could say she was dancing in a lustful manner.

This chapter is about the kind of dancing that goes on at your high school or middle school dance.

What Does The Bible Say About Dancing?

Chances are, you probably didn't know that there is any condemnation of dancing in the Bible. In fact, you may have even used that as an argument in favor of dancing. Several of my friends have said, "Nowhere in the Bible does it say, "Thou shalt not dance." What I am about to show you, however, may surprise you.

Galatians 5:19-21 says, "Now the works of the flesh are manifest, which are these; adultery, fornication, uncleanness, lasciviousness, idolatry, witchcraft, hatred, variance, emulations, wrath, strife, seditions, heresies, envyings, murders, drunkenness, revellings, and such like: of which I tell you before, as I have also told you in time past, that they which do such things shall not inherit the kingdom of God."

Look at the word "lasciviousness." This may be the first time you have heard this word. It is not often that, when we go on a date, our moms say, "Have a good time and don't be lascivious!" before we leave. It is just no longer a word we use. So what did God mean by that word? The Greek word for "lasciviousness" is *aselgeia*. According to Thayer's Greek Lexicon, one of the definitions of *aselgeia* is, "Wanton manners as filthy words, indecent bodily movements, unchaste handling of males and females..." Read that definition again. What does that remind you of? It should remind you of the prom, the eighth grade dance, the homecoming dance, etc...

I talked with one mom recently who was upset about what had gone on at her son's middle school dance. Her son came home and told her that there were seventh and eighth graders committing fornication in the corners of the gym while the dance was going on. She could not believe that something like that would happen at such a prestigious and academically upstanding school. I hate to be blunt, but when you fill a gym with pre-teens and teens, turn the lights down low, and encourage them to rub their bodies against each other to the slow rhythm of seductive music, what do you expect? If it isn't a slow song, it's an upbeat one where one will move her body in front of her partner while that partner looks on and does the same. Call me radical, but if this kind of dancing that goes on at the prom, and other such dances, is not "unchaste handling of males and females; indecent bodily movement" I am interested to know what is. Frankly, I cannot think of anything that better fits the description, "indecent bodily movement" than modern-day dancing.

In that particular passage, God does not just say, "Try to avoid these things." He says, "They which do such things shall not inherit the kingdom of God." I don't know about you, but I don't want to risk my salvation over a few school dances. It's really not worth it.

Another part of that passage that catches my eye is the words, "and such like." That means that, as a Christian, I should stay as far from the sins listed in this passage as possible. In today's society, what (besides dancing) might involve lasciviousness? The way we dress, our dating behavior, the CDs we listen to, and the movies we watch can all cause us to be lascivious. Please remember the definition of lascivious as you reflect on those things in other chapters of this book.

Is This Dancing, Too?

One form of dancing is difficult for me to address because it is so popular, even among many Christians. It is called cheerleading. I realize that it is not like this in every school, but in most cases, cheerleading is a lascivious activity. The skirts come far above the knee and they come up frequently during flips, cartwheels, etc., to reveal what is no more modest than skimpy underwear. There is usually a tease line between the skirt and top, and sometimes the entire stomach is revealed. I don't have to tell you this. You know. Not only are these girls extremely immodest, but also most of the movements they make are lascivious. The movements go anywhere from swinging hips to shaking chests, but these movements are provoking lust in the opposite sex, whether we girls realize it or not. In a way, cheerleading is worse than dancing. At dances, a girl moves her body in front of one guy. At the ball games, a girl moves her body in front of a large audience as a form of entertainment. Girls, what are we thinking?!

Please don't misunderstand me. I think cheering for your favorite team is a wonderful thing to do, but we can cheer just as well with all of our clothes on and without indecent movements! Perhaps, most of the time, we will just have to cheer from the bleachers instead of on the sidelines.

What Am I Going To Do About It?

Once you know the definition of lasciviousness, and once you have really thought about dancing in this light, you have to decide whether or not you choose to participate. There is no straddling the fence. Yes, you will be different, or even weird, because you do not involve yourself in the activities of your friends, but it will be worth it. Standing up for what you believe in now will help you grow by leaps and bounds. But that is not the best part. The best part is that you will be rewarded one day for the stand you take now, and you will be so glad you took that stand!

It will take lots of sacrifice. I have tried to talk several of my friends out of going to the prom, and I always hear the words, "You only get one chance to go to your senior prom."

That's true, but let's look at the flip side of that. You only get one chance to stand up and say "No" to your senior prom. That's all. After you have gone to the prom (or any other dance for that matter), you will never have that chance again. You will never be able to sacrifice that particular special evening for the one who sacrificed His own life for you. Christianity is meant to be a sacrifice. Romans 12:1-2 says, "I beseech you therefore, brethren, by the mercies of God, that ye present your bodies a living sacrifice, holy, acceptable unto God, which is your reasonable service. And be not conformed to this world: but be ye transformed by the renewing of your mind, that ye may prove what is that good, and acceptable, and perfect, will of God."

I beg you to seriously consider your views on dancing, remembering what the Bible says about it, and, as Christian girls, let's show our true colors by choosing more holy forms of recreation. "Be ye holy for I am holy" (I Peter 1:16).

Questions:

1. Should the fact that the whole world thinks dancing is acceptable affect my view of dancing as a Christian? Find one or more New Testament verses that tell us that our thinking should be different from the thinking of the world.

2. Are there other biblical examples of dancing? Find one in the New Testament in which a girl's dance ultimately cost a man his head.

3. In Mark 7:21-23, what does the scripture say will happen to someone who is lascivious?

4. According to II Corinthians 12:21, what should we do if we have been lascivious?

5. In what list is lasciviousness found in Galatians 5:19?

6. In what condition are we when we "have given ourselves over unto lasciviousness" (Ephesians 4:19)?

7. From I Peter 4:1-4, how will others perceive us if we avoid things like lasciviousness?

8. How does Jude 4 describe men who "turn the grace of our God into lasciviousness?"

9. Give an example of lascivious behavior portrayed in the media. Explain how we can avoid these portrayals of lasciviousness and other temptations the media may present.

10. For what two reasons is cheerleading generally sinful?

11. Think of great alternatives for groups of Christian teens to do together on prom night. Examples: Formal dinner banquet with music and professional photographer or a weekend youth trip to a great destination complete with lots of devos and snacks.

Projects:

1. Study the Greek definition of the word "lasciviousness" and make a list of all daily activities that could become lascivious, and how they could come to be that way.After you've made this list, write an essay on lasciviousness, and conclude the essay with a pledge that you will abstain from doing the things you've written about (don't say it unless you mean it!). Read this aloud at the next meeting.

2. Find a story in the Bible about someone, or a group of people, who had to face a lot of trouble and heartache because of someone's sin of lasciviousness. Write an essay on this Biblical example and read it aloud at the next meeting.

3. Plan a prom alternative for your youth group and their friends. You may have to plan this far in advance. Talk to someone in charge of youth at your congregation about setting a date, and begin organizing the events of that special night or weekend.

4. An additional problem with attending the prom tends to be activities that occur following the dance. List these activities in two columns: the sinful activities and the activities that are wholesome. Which list is longer? Find scriptures to show that each of the activities in the first column would not be pleasing to God. Bring this list to the next meeting.

5. Re-read the previous lesson on modest dress. Go to the Juniors formal department of a store in your local mall. Look through the dresses on a rack and rate each one on a scale of 1-10, with 10 being modest beyond question and 1 being a prostitute's outfit. When you have done this activity, reflect on typical prom wear an decide if you think the dress at most proms is lascivious.

6. Plan a teen girls class on the subject of dancing. Either teach this class or invite someone to prepare this lesson and present it. Allow the girls to ask questions at
   the end of the session.

Works Cited

Most of the material in this chapter was taken from Hannah Colley. *"Dancing."* in *Girl To Girl.* Ed. Laura Elliott. Huntsville, AL, Publishing Designs, 2005

CHAPTER EIGHT:
Life Savings

A lady in my community opened up about her teenage step-daughter who not only has sex with multiple partners, but sells tickets for other teenagers to come over and watch. The girl also sells nude pictures of herself on the internet, and participates in "cyber sex" regularly. The girl is only 14 years old, and all this is going on in the home of this lady I know.

A fun autumn fieldtrip recently was planned for the 7th grade class of a prestigious middle school in a little Alabama town. The group had to leave the hay maze early because they couldn't control the oral sex that was occurring throughout the maze among the middle school students. These days, most people aren't surprised to hear that oral sex is a favorite pastime among middle school students.

A blood drive occurred recently in another small town. 50% of the high school students who were responsible enough to volunteer to give blood tested HIV positive.

We live in a pretty sick society. In most high schools, the really good girls are the ones who typically have sex with only one partner, and even those seem to be rare. Today, more than ever, we as teenage girls have a difficult battle to fight.

Sex isn't supposed to be something ugly. God created it, and it is a precious gift when used within the beautiful realm of marriage. However, it becomes ugly when people casually misuse the gift by participating in sexual activity outside of that God-approved union (Hebrews 13:4).

Sexual purity is something to cherish and hold, and someday present to the person for whom we've been saving it and protecting it. This is God's plan for us (I Corinthians 6:18). However, we need to keep in mind that our God is a God of forgiveness. You may be someone who has already made the mistake of letting go of your purity. If you have repented, God will forgive you. This does not mean that you will never face consequences because of your sin, but it does mean that you can find peace, happiness, and, most importantly, the joy of forgiveness in Christ. Paul reminded the Corinthians that they were once involved in the most vile forms of sexual sin (I Corinthians 6:9-10), but then assured them that, "...you are washed, you are sanctified, you are justified in the name of the Lord Jesus" (I Corinthians 6:11).

As I was writing this chapter, I wondered why it seems there are so many more consequences involved with sexual sin than with many other sins. I mean, think about it; unwanted pregnancy, sexually transmitted diseases, struggling marriages, and the general disdain from many people around you. Why is sexual sin so consequential?

I Corinthians 6:18 reads, "Flee fornication. Every sin that a man doeth is without the body; but he that committeth fornication sinneth against his own body."

Evidently, sexual sin is much more difficult to get past than all other sins. This chapter will hopefully help you realize the importance of sexual purity, and encourage you to hold on to that precious gift God has given you.

Two Biblical Examples: Flee Or Fall

Genesis 39 tells us about a time when Joseph had to deal with the temptation of fornication. Joseph worked for a very powerful, authoritative man named Potiphar. He was Potiphar's most trusted servant (Genesis 39:3, 4). Verse 6 tells us that Joseph was very good looking. While Potiphar was away from home, Potiphar's wife made several attempts to get Joseph to sleep with her. Every day, he refused her desperate attempts. Verse 10 reads, "And it came to pass, as she spake to Joseph day by day, that he hearkened not unto her, to lie with her, or to be with her."

One day, as Joseph was working in the house, Potiphar's wife thought she could get him this time, since the two of them were the only people in the house (Genesis 39:11). She took hold of his coat and once again, begged him to sleep with her (verse 12). Joseph didn't waste any time. He got out of that coat she was holding, and ran.

When we read the rest of the story, we see that Joseph was falsely accused of rape, and sent to prison. However, we also see that, in spite of Joseph's rotten luck, God stayed with him, and eventually blessed him with so much more than he had before.

Joseph could have said, "Oh, Mrs. Potiphar, I would really like to make love with you. You're so beautiful. Why don't we sit down and talk about this, though. This probably isn't such a good idea." Even better, he could have said, "Why don't we pray about this together?" He didn't do either of those things though. Verse 12 said he "left his garment in her hand, and fled, and got him out." When we're faced with the temptation of fornication, we don't think about it. We don't talk about it. We don't pray about it. We GET OUTTA THERE. Saturate that place with your absence. When you do this, you will save yourself from a lot of heartache and many problems. We see this when we look at II Samuel 11 where we read about someone who didn't "flee."

King David had decided to take the day off from going to battle with his men, and take it easy in Jerusalem. Some say that if David had not let laziness get in his way of traveling with his men to battle, the sin would not have occurred. Perhaps he had a good reason to stay at home. However, we do know that he was relaxing, because verse 2 tells us he arose from his bed at eventide (or dusk) and climbed to his roof. As he was gazing at the acres and acres of land which he owned, something very appealing caught his eye: a beautiful woman bathing. Some scholars say this was a common occurrence; others say that's very unlikely.

Anyway, David's eyes lingered on this bathing beauty appropriately named Bathsheba, which was a sin in itself. But he didn't stop there. He sent messengers to go and get her and bring her to him. Verse 4 tells us, "…[David] took her; and she came in unto him, and he lay with her." We can assume that David did this knowing that she was another man's wife. Her husband's name was Uriah. He was one of David's chief warriors. Verses 6 and 7 indicate that Uriah must have held some office of authority, because David sent to him to inquire about the battle that took place while he was sleeping with his wife.

Not long after that, Bathsheba went and told David she was pregnant with his child. David panicked, and immediately formulated a plan. His first move was to try to persuade Uriah to go home for the night and sleep with his wife so that it could easily be assumed that the child was Uriah's. Uriah did the noble thing, however, and refused to go home while the rest of the men were out fighting. He slept on David's door step that night.

David proceeded to get Uriah drunk the following day. He told him once again to go home to his wife. Evidently, Uriah still had enough sense to refuse. He spent another night at the door of David's house.

It seems as though David ran out of good ideas. He decided he would simply have Uriah killed. He sent a letter to Joab demanding him to place Uriah at the front of the battle, then to desert him so Uriah would be killed instantly. He had the audacity to send this letter using Uriah himself as messenger.

After Uriah's death, many tribulations haunted David because of his sin. The child conceived by Bathsheba died as punishment. David went through a lot of emotional torture. We can read about his anguish and repentance in Psalm 51.

God forgave David, but just look at all of the horrible things that occurred because of David's sin.

Why Should I Wait?

At the time I wrote this book, I'd never been married before, but I'd learned a lot about marriage by talking to women like my mother. Saving your purity for the man you will one day marry is how God intended it to be. As a teen, I knew that when I walked down that aisle someday in the presence of my family and friends, I wanted to give my husband my whole life's savings. This choice is romantic. This choice is responsible. But most of all, it's respectful. It's respectful of my husband and the One who created this whole thing called marriage in the first place.

My parents have counseled many people who are having so many problems in their marriages. Many of these people admit that their marriages would be so much better if they had just done things God's way and remained pure before they married. It's very difficult for people who have had sex with multiple partners to be satisfied sexually with their spouses. Many people struggle with this.

Marriage is truly wonderful if you can discover the beauty of sex simply by being unified for the first time with the man with whom you want to spend the rest of your life.

Consider a rose just beginning to bloom. It's fresh, pure, and beautiful. It's a lovely gift to give someone special, but only if it's been handled carefully. If you've passed it around to all of your friends to let them touch and handle it before giving it as a gift, it's not as good when you're ready to present it. It's wrinkled, flimsy, spotted, and falling apart. That's how sex is. If you've passed it around to other people, it's not a complete and perfect gift anymore.

Even though I hadn't met him yet when I wrote this book, I loved my future husband enough to save everything I had just for him, and it was so worth it. I wouldn't let anyone harm the gift I was saving for him.

How Can I Wait?

There are many ways that we, as girls, can guard ourselves from sexual temptation, as well as help our guy friends to abstain. We have to be careful that we are not only abstaining from sex itself, but also abstaining from the things that may lead to sex, or the things that encourage sexual thoughts. For example, a girl shouldn't sit in a guy's lap. I know that sounds funny, but, while we may not think anything of it, it's very difficult for a guy not to think about you sexually when you're sitting in his lap. What are some other practical ways we can abstain?

What About Kissing?

My mother recently taught a teenage girls Bible class in which I was a student. One of my friends asked, "Is French kissing wrong to do before you get married?" Mom wasn't sure what to say, so she came home that night and asked my dad what he thought about it. He replied, "There is no way that a guy can engage in something like that without thinking sexual thoughts about the girl participating."

When a guy takes you home after a date, a kiss should mean, "Goodnight," not "Come in, Honey."

What About Hugging?

This one is especially tough for me, because I am a hugging person. I love to hug my friends! It wasn't until recently that my dad and my brother opened my eyes to what may be going through the minds of my guy friends when I participate in a full-frontal hug. It is very hard for guys to keep from thinking about you in a sexual way when we give them long, tight, frontal hugs. Try distant hugs with guys, or even side hugs. You can't go wrong there! ☺

What About Touching?

We need to wake up and realize that areas that are not for looking are definitely not for touching. I'm not saying it's wrong when a guy pats you on the back. But we know the difference between an innocent pat on the back and lascivious touching. We must draw serious lines somewhere between the two. Here are some examples from my personal set of dating standards:

No hands on inner thighs
No back rubs…his mom can do that for him.
No prolonged undisturbed periods of time alone together.
I could go on, but you get the point. Standards should be set early on.

We can't decide, "I'm going to be pure," without setting some guidelines for ourselves. Make some rules for yourself and try writing them down.

A Modern-Day Example Of The Consequences Of Sexual Sin

This story was contributed by a friend of mine who recently became a New Testament Christian:

"I grew up hearing that any boy who truly loves you will not pressure you to have sex. This is not a completely true statement. Unfortunately, I learned it the hard way. I started dating at fifteen. We spent a good amount of time together over the next several months. We held hands, hugged, and even kissed a few times. I was pretty sure that this was the person I was going to marry. I was so sure that when his hand moved from my back to my side I didn't think twice. As a matter of fact, I didn't feel any regret or remorse when things moved to touching. We were in love.

Eventually he got frustrated with me and began pressuring me to "go all the way". I didn't feel that I was emotionally ready, nor did I love him that much so I dumped him.

My next boyfriend promised me that he would not pressure me to have sex. I'll give him credit that he never did. I willingly consented every step of the way. Because we were in love I rarely questioned if what we were doing was wrong. I knew that the Bible said that fornication is a sin, but we were going to get married so it was probably fine that we went ahead and had sex. I later broke up with him and continued this pattern for two years.

I got pregnant with my first child when I was nineteen. My baby's dad broke up with me because I refused to have an abortion. Nine months after my daughter was born I married her dad; not her biological father, but the man who is raising her.

I would like to tell you from my position as someone who did choose to have sex outside of marriage how very deep the emotional scars run. God has forgiven me, but that doesn't mean that he took the consequences of fornication away. Every week I have to turn my child over to someone who stands for everything that I hate. He is not a Christian and certainly acts accordingly. My daughter got hurt in a basketball game and he told her, "One cigarette and a beer and you'll feel much better.

More than the pain and frustration of dealing with her father, his many girlfriends, and juvenile court is the pain of knowing that I so casually, carelessly, and repeatedly offended God. I could never fully put into words the sadness that I feel when I look back at what I've done to myself and others.

I once asked a leader at the "church" I went to as a teen, "How far is too far?" The response was, "Well, what is too far for me may be just fine for you." The worst lie I ever believed! God did not give us strong sexual desire and no clear boundaries for controlling those desires. Satan wants us to believe that there are no real issues of dating so he can break into our defenses step by step."

Questions:

1. Discuss some sexual activities that are occurring with people in your school or in your social circles and ways we can avoid participating in those activities.

2. Find at least three verses in the Bible (besides those mentioned in this chapter) about fleeing fornication or about the sin of sex outside of marriage.

3. Discuss ways that we can avoid sexual temptation.

4. What sins are listed in I Corinthians 6:9-11 in which the phrase "... and such were some of you" is used?

5. Give other examples of Bible characters who faced sexual temptation.

6. List the consequences of David's sexual sin.

Projects

1. Enlarge this purity pledge and copy it on cardstock for each member. Have each girl sit down and study the scriptures included with her mother or an adult mentor who will help her keep the pledge. Have both sign the pledge. Each class member should display the pledge in her room.

My Promise of Purity

Because He is my Creator, and knows what's best for me (Psalm 100:3), and because He loved me enough to give His Son that I might have life (John 3:16; John 20:30-31),

I will keep my heart pure, for I want to see Him (Matthew 5:8), and I will keep my body pure, because it is my living sacrifice to Him (Romans 12:1).

I _____ promise before God and this witness that I will refrain from sexual activity until I enter a God-approved marriage (Hebrews 13:4).

Signed _____

Witness _____

Date _____

2. Re-write the story of Joseph. What do you think would have happened in his life and the lives of his family if he had given in to sexual temptation? What would have happened to Egypt?

3. Design a calligraphy on pretty parchment of Psalm 51:10. Frame this and hang it in your room. Show this to your mentor. Speak with a Christian marriage counselor about problems in marriages that result from sexual sin before marriage. List the resultant problems he encounters in counseling.

4. Plan a seminar for your community's teens. Have a qualified person give abstinence counseling and show the dangers of so called "safe sex." Invite parents to attend, as well.

5. Plan a teen girl's purity day. After you've received approval from the elders of your congregation, invite a speaker to come talk about sexual purity. Design pretty invitations and send them out to all of your girl friends. Each girl must participate in a leadership role, such as leading a song or prayer, or reading scripture, in order to count this as one of her projects.

6. Write a research paper on teen sex in America. Footnote all sources. Include a bibliography. Submit this to your mentor.

CHAPTER NINE:
Hello?! It's Just Entertainment

Everybody loves entertainment. Opinions and preferences differ, but when it comes right down to it, we all love to be entertained. As Christians, however, we must carefully consider whether our entertainment choices are pleasing to God.

This chapter will cover the influence entertainment has on us, and what we can do about it.

The Bible And Mind Control

When we hear the words, "mind control," we automatically sense a negative connotation. Mind control is a bad thing, if mere people are controlling our minds. However, when we allow God to control our minds, it's always a good thing. God wants us to allow Him to rule every part of us. Luke 10:27 reads, "...Thou shalt love the Lord thy God with all thy heart, and with all thy soul, and with all thy strength, and with all thy mind..."

God wants us to love Him completely and totally. How can we show this love? I Corinthians 13:6 reads, "[Love] rejoiceth not in iniquity but rejoiceth in the truth."

In reference to entertainment, when I laugh at something sinful or pay money to see or listen to something sinful, I am rejoicing in iniquity. God wants us to avoid this. How should this self-sacrificing love affect my thoughts?

Philippians 4:8 reads, "Finally, brethren, whatsoever things are true, whatsoever things are honest, whatsoever things are just, whatsoever things are pure, whatsoever things are lovely, whatsoever things are of good report; if there be any virtue, and if there be any praise, think on these things."

God wants us to stay focused on good things, rather than evil things. In Psalm 19:14 David prayed, "Let the words of my mouth and the meditation of my heart be acceptable in thy sight, O Lord, my strength, and my redeemer."

This needs to be our prayer, as well. Our desire needs to be to keep our hearts and minds clean and unspotted by the world.

The Media And The Mind

Some may say, "Oh, what I see on television and what I hear on the radio doesn't affect me." I highly doubt the validity of such a statement. If that's true about the majority of people, then why do businesses pay millions of dollars to have a 30 second commercial play during the Super Bowl? Obviously, media has the ability to influence the way we think.

It's sad to notice that many people believe that if Hollywood produces it, we have to see it. Many Christians have fallen into this mindset. Often, this is inconsistent with the way they live as Christians. They feel completely at ease watching and hearing sinful things as long as it's coming from the television or from a movie screen.

For the sake of illustration, let's say I'm babysitting small children, and we're playing in front of a large bay window. What if I looked out the window and noticed that right there on the front lawn, two people were committing fornication. What would I do? Would I say, "Hey, kids! Let's watch!" Of course not. Unless I'm a psycho, I would immediately close the blinds to protect them from witnessing that. I should close them to protect me, as well.

Many people have such a window right in their living rooms, and yet so many of us just leave it open, regardless of what we see through that window. I'm shocked at Christians who would be appalled if someone came in their houses and began cursing, making sexual innuendos, or making fun of God. They would send that person right out of their homes and ask him never to return. But if it's happening on the television, they don't do anything about it.

We need to stop kidding ourselves and close the window. I Thessalonians 5:22 reads, "Abstain from every appearance of evil."

That simply means, keep your eyes away from everything that's evil. What kind of evil entertainment should I avoid? We need to steer clear of movies and music that include sexuality, things that mock God, and bad language. This is so hard because almost everything on these days is full of these things. It means sacrifice.

Many people try to cover up their sin of making bad entertainment choices by using excuses like these:

"There was nothing else on!" Guess what? There ARE other options. There is such a thing as an OFF button on your television. Find something better to do than sit and mindlessly stare at a screen if you can't find something innocent on which to feast your mind.

"The plot was so good other than a few dirty parts, so I watched it anyway."

Let's say that I'm having a party at my house, and when all my friends arrive, I open the oven and pull out some hot, gooey brownies. My friends gather around and say, "Mmm...those smell so good! We can't wait to try them! What's your recipe?" I begin describing all the ingredients that make up my lovely treat.

"Flour, sugar, eggs, milk, lots of chocolate...and just a little tiny bit of dog poop." Do you think they're going to want to eat my brownies now? But it's only a teaspoon of poop! The rest of the ingredients are so good, you won't even taste it. Don't you think they can just overlook that one thing? Of course not. If you wouldn't use this logic in reference to what you're feeding your stomach, would you want to use that logic in reference to what you're feeding your soul--the part of you that will live for eternity? I hope not.

"That's all my friends talk about! If I don't watch the shows and movies they watch, I will be totally left out." That's GREAT. Give yourself a pat on the back if you're left out of this situation, because you will be able to do two things for Christ:

First, you will be abstaining from the appearance of evil when your friends see it and you don't, and secondly, you won't be involved in talking about that impurity after they've watched it.

We need to ask ourselves a couple of questions before we allow ourselves to be entertained. Are there any appearances of evil in what I'm watching (I Thessalonians 5:22)? If Jesus Himself walked in the door and sat in the seat right beside me, would I continue watching what I'm watching? We need to remember that He is there, every minute of every day.

What Can I Do About It?

What are some ways that I can avoid letting Satan get in my way of serving God with a pure heart? Here are some suggestions:

Use the Internet. Type in Google the name of the movie you want to watch, then "parental review." There are several websites that include just about every movie Hollywood has put out in the past 20 years, as well as all recent releases, and provide a list of all possible offensive words and scenes in each movie. By visiting these websites, you will know exactly what you'll be watching before you watch it. This tool has really helped my family to know whether watching certain movies is a waste of money before we waste the money. ☺

Buy a television filter such as TV Guardian or ClearPlay. I have a TV Guardian. This is one of the coolest things I have in my house. I promise it's worth the money. TV Guardian is something you hook up to your television, and every time someone curses, it mutes the sentence and has subtitles at the bottom of the screen, changing the offensive word to something clean. This is one way you can enjoy those great plots without having to hear all the profanity. TV Guardians can be purchased at most Wal-Marts, or you can order it online at www.tvguardian.com,

Clean out your movie shelf and your CD shelf/iPod. Put the trash where it belongs. Try finding a faithful Christian of your congregation and have him or her listen to some of your music and help you know with which songs you should use the "skip" button. While it's good to have other people help you to be what you need to be, remember that nobody can make your mind up for you. YOU have to decide that you're going to keep your thoughts pure by abstaining from evil entertainment.

In conclusion, let's consider one more thing. If there was no such thing as the internet, movies, television, music, magazines, books, and any other forms of entertainment, could we still get to heaven? Of course. It's just entertainment. We can live without it all and still go to heaven. If your choices of entertainment are what are keeping you outside the will of Christ, there are several ways to select pure entertainment instead. But if it's still an issue for you, give it up! It's just entertainment.

May God bless you as you strive to make better choices of entertainment for the sake of Christ.

Questions:

1. Find at least two verses pertaining to our thoughts that are not mentioned in this chapter.

2. Think of some excuses you've heard in reference to sinful entertainment and discuss these in class. Think of good, Biblical responses to these excuses.

3. Visit www.kids-in-mind.com and read about at least two movies that you have been considering going to see at the movie theater. Be honest with yourself in deciding whether this is something a Christian should be watching.

4. Have you ever considered the fact that Jesus is sitting beside you every time you watch television? How does that affect you?

5. What's another good reason, besides those given in this lesson, to be left out of going to see bad movies with your friends?

6. Make a list of the dangers of unprotected internet use.

Projects

1. Clean out all movie and CD shelves. Throw away the things you know are inappropriate. Write an essay on why you did this, and how it has helped you and will help you. Read the essay at the next meeting.

2. Contact the American Family Association. Find out how you can join in the campaign to clean up our media. Visit www.afa.net.

3. Research the basis for movie ratings. What triggers a PG-13 rating? How many dirty words before a PG-13 rating becomes an R rating? Bring the information you find to the next meeting.

4. Make a list of at least twenty verses that teach us about guarding our thought processes. Memorize 10 of these and quote them to your mentor.

5. Share this lesson about entertainment choices with at least five of your friends that need to hear it. Make sure you do this with a caring and humble attitude. The author gives permission to photocopy the chapter for this project.

6. Do some research on the different kinds of internet filters available. If you don't already have one, I strongly encourage you to get one. Also, go to your Preferences or Settings and figure out how you can block dirty emails from being sent to your inbox. Work on this before the next meeting.

7. Pledge that, for one month, you will switch the channel or turn off the TV every time you hear sexual innuendos or jokes, profanity, or gutter talk.

CHAPTER TEN:
The Real High

Part 1: Drinking

We've all read bumper stickers or billboards that say "Don't drink and drive," or "Friends don't let friends drive drunk," but we rarely hear people say negative things about drinking at times other than when someone's behind the wheel. It's a social activity in which most people participate. Eight out of every ten high school seniors have tried it. So, what's the big deal? This chapter will address the issue which most people consider a non-issue.

Inspiration

First, let's take a look at what God has to say about drinking:

Proverbs 20:1: "Wine is a mocker, strong drink is raging: and whosoever is deceived thereby is not wise."

Isaiah 5:22, 23, "Woe unto them that are mighty to drink wine, and men of strength to mingle strong drink: Which justify the wicked for reward, and take away the righteousness of the righteous from him!"

I Thessalonians 5: 7, 8, "...they that be drunken are drunken in the night, but let us, who are of the day, be sober, putting on the breastplate of faith and love; and for an helmet, the hope of salvation."

Galatians 5:19, 21, "Now the works of the flesh are manifest, which are these; ...Envyings, murders, drunkenness, revellings, and such like: of the which I tell you before, as I have also told you in time past, that they which do such things shall not enter the kingdom of God."

Intoxication

The passages above indicate that God is vehemently opposed to us getting drunk. They all put drinking in a very negative light. The clearest one in my mind is the last one—Galatians 5:19, 21. This is a list of actions that will prevent us from entering the kingdom of heaven, one of which is drunkenness. Did you get that? Getting drunk will keep us from going to heaven! Gone unforgiven, one night of that kind of "fun" can affect an eternity.

Besides the obvious reasons not to get drunk, evidence proves that alcohol slows down the mind and the body, even after we've suffered the immediate side effects. With each drink, you're destroying brain cells, which may slow down your thinking and reasoning abilities for the rest of your life. The following statistics are the percentage of students reporting having experienced each of the following potential consequences of drinking during the year prior to completing the Core survey in 2001: 64.5% had a hangover. 24.4% performed poorly on a test or other project. 16.5% had trouble with police or other authorities. 31.8% got into an argument or fight. 55.3% got nauseated or vomited. 29% drove a car while under the influence. 34.1% missed a class. 34.7% suffered from memory loss. 40.5% did something they later regretted.

I recently talked with a friend who regretted having become drunk a few months prior to our conversation. He said that he never liked the taste of alcohol, but that he was pressured to drink it at this certain party, and he was a little depressed anyway, so he drank until he was beyond tipsy. He felt awful for at least an entire week after that one night. He didn't do well in school, and he felt like a slob. He couldn't enjoy his regular social activities due to that one night of drinking.

This is all very disturbing, but let's remember that statistics and stories aren't really important. The main thing is that God said it. That's all that matters. Drunkenness is clearly prohibited by God under any circumstances. That doesn't mean that he doesn't want us to have any fun. He isn't saying, "I want you to commit social suicide." He's saying "I don't want you to get hurt. Please take care of your body, my temple."

Moderation

I was talking to a friend the other day about her beliefs about drinking. She had come to the decision that to get drunk was an unhealthy choice. She has big dreams and wild ambition is written all over her face. She figured, with all the statistics about the physical harm done by getting drunk, that excessive drinking might hold her back from doing what she wanted to do. However, she had no problem with drinking occasionally, and in small amounts. "I'll still drink beer at parties or whatever, but I'm scared that, if I get drunk all the time, my talents will be hurt by it."

My first mental response was "You go girl." But then I thought, if each drink destroys brain cells, and it does, then her logic is flawed. If a lot of alcohol does a lot of harm, then a moderate amount of alcohol would do a moderate amount of harm. We know from multiple passages of Scripture that God despises drunkenness. What, though, in God's mind, is drunk? Can anyone say for sure? No. God didn't define it. He didn't give us a blood-alcohol content level. So, for all we know, "drunk" could possibly mean "having been altered to any degree by the drink." We cannot know for sure what God meant by the word "drunk," so it's wise just to completely avoid it.

This is not the only reason not to drink. There is also a pressing influence issue. Even if you only intend to drink occasionally and in very small amounts, the people who see you buying or accepting the beverage will assume you participate in and endorse the use of alcoholic beverages. If you want to encourage others (young people, perhaps) to abstain from drunkenness, you will not be seen purchasing any alcoholic beverages. How could you possibly teach others that drunkenness is a sin when they have seen you buying or perhaps drinking a glass of beer or wine? You will lose that precious opportunity to influence.

A few years ago I happened upon one of the teenagers from the congregation where we attended at that time. He was hanging out with some other teens in a parking lot. As my family drove by and waved hello, we noticed him passing a beer to the guy sitting beside him. I didn't know for sure that he was drinking with them, but if he ever tried to discourage me from doing it, I wouldn't be apt to listen after that. Perhaps that seems extreme, but I'm just being honest with you. That's how people react, whether or not they know all the facts. Let's make sure that our influence is the very best it can be in every single setting and situation.

I can't make choices about alcohol for you. You have to decide for yourself. I do want to remind you of something, though. Even if you just drink a little now and then but plan to be through with alcohol by the time you have kids, you will regret drinking one day. I know parents who are so afraid when they talk to their kids about drinking and drugs. They're afraid of the question, "Dad (or Mom), did you ever drink?" Don't make choices now that will require you to look your child in the eye one day and say, "Yes, I did." Your ability to keep them away from alcohol may be forfeited. Children often feel it is okay to do something their parents have done. That fact has been proven throughout all of time. We even see several biblical examples of this.

For these and other reasons, we, as Christian girls, will be wise if we choose to abstain from any form of drinking. God will bless us for it!

One final thought: Alcoholism is, by all standards, a major problem in our society. But think about this. If everyone in America agreed with the points I've made about completely avoiding alcohol, the problem would not exist. No drunk driver accidents. No accidental alcohol/ drug overdoses. No hungry children whose livelihood is spent on the drink. No hangover. No alcohol induced liver disease. Why would this be the case? Think about these two statements: First, no one who refused to experiment with alcohol ever became an alcoholic. Even those who may have strong genetic predispositions to be alcoholics will not become alcoholics if they avoid the first drink. Second, there are many alcoholics who never intended to become such when they took their first drinks.

Conclusion

There are several choices regarding alcohol use. Among them are total abstinence, social drinking, private drinking, and excessive drinking. There is only one safe choice for Christians.

Part 2: Drugs

"Come on. Just try it. This will take away all the stress and make you feel ten times better. If you just do it once, it can't hurt you."

Sound familiar? These same words have been used millions of times on gullible teenagers who often fall into the trap.

Is there a verse in the Bible that says, "Don't do drugs"? Well, no. But there are many about taking care of our bodies, which are temples for the Lord. I Corinthians 6:19, 20 reads,

"What? Know ye not that your body is the temple of the Holy Ghost which is in you, which ye have of God, and ye are not your own? For ye are bought with a price: therefore glorify God in your body, and in your spirit, which are God's."

Romans 6:12, 13 reads,

"Let not sin therefore reign in your mortal body, that ye should obey it in the lusts thereof. Neither yield ye your members as instruments of righteousness unto sin: but yield yourselves unto God, as those that are alive from the dead, and your members as instruments of righteousness unto God."

Romans 12:1 reads,

"I beseech you therefore, brethren, by the mercies of God, that you present your bodies a living sacrifice, holy, acceptable unto God, which is your reasonable service."

So, what's so bad about using drugs? Let's look at some different popular harmful drugs, and the effects they have on their victims.

Among teenagers, the most commonly used drugs are tobacco and alcohol. Yes, these are drugs. Many parents back away from addressing these issues because they are too busy fearing that their children will become interested in the "harder drugs." Evidence shows that two out of three teenagers have tried smoking. Tobacco smoking causes more deaths than any other drug. Tobacco smoke contains more that 4000 chemicals, including:

- Tar (a mixture of chemicals)
- Nicotine (an addictive substance)
- Carbon monoxide (found in car exhaust fumes)
- Ammonia (found in floor cleaner)
- Arsenic (found in rat poison)

At least 60 of the chemicals in tobacco smoke are known to cause cancer. Smoking causes cancer of the lung, throat, mouth, bladder, and kidneys.

Nicotine is the drug that makes tobacco smokers want to keep on smoking. Research has shown that nicotine, like heroin, is highly addictive. Research shows that most tobacco smokers want to quit, and have tried. The process of breaking the habit involves symptoms such as:

- Cravings
- Irritability, frustration, depression and/or anxiety
- Restlessness
- Difficulty concentrating
- Changed sleeping patterns
- Increase in appetite and weight gain
- Coughing

It is important to realize that legal drugs can be every bit as harmful as illegal drugs.

Marijuana is the most commonly used illegal drug among teenagers. It can be smoked or eaten and comes in a variety of forms such as dried plant leaves and flowers, a crumbly light brown or dark brown resinous material called "hash" or in the form of a very strong oil, called "hash oil." Marijuana is a depressant drug which slows down the central nervous system and the messages going to and from the brain to the body.

The immediate effects of small doses of marijuana, or cannabis, last approximately two to three hours and can include:

- A sense of well-being
- Reduced concentration
- Decreased coordination
- Distorted perceptions of time, space, and distance
- Increased heart rate
- Drowsiness
- Increased appetite
- Reddened eyes

Larger doses or stronger forms of marijuana make these effects stronger and add other effects like:

- Confusion
- Restlessness
- Feelings of excitement
- Hallucinations
- Anxiety or panic
- Detachment from reality
- Paranoia
- Nausea

Long-term marijuana users may experience additional effects including:

* The risk of asthma, emphysema, shortness of breath, chest infections, and throat, mouth, and lung cancers.

* Poor concentration, memory loss, and learning difficulties.

* Depression of the immune system, which increases the risk of developing infections.

* Serious mental illness, such as schizophrenia.

Cocaine is an illegal stimulant drug extracted from the leaves of the coca plant and processed with a blend of other chemicals to form a white powder known as cocaine hydrochloride. This type of cocaine is typically inhaled or injected. Since cocaine hydrochloride is mixed with other chemicals, the user generally has no idea if the dose will be strong or weak.

"Crack" cocaine is processed differently and can be smoked. Common slang for this form includes "coke," "blow," and "stardust."

Upon dosage of cocaine, the brain "rewards" us for engaging in life enhancing behavior, such as eating, by releasing a flood of pleasurable neurochemicals. Dopamine is one of these brain chemicals. This chemical's reinforcement makes us want to engage in those behaviors again and again.

Cocaine works by tapping into this reward system and triggering the release of dopamine. This is what makes cocaine extremely addictive.

The effects of cocaine depend on the strength of the dose, the blend of the chemicals, the physiology of the user and her state of mind at the time of taking the drug. The cocaine rush only lasts 15 minutes to half an hour after inhalation. Generally, some of the immediate effects include:

- Feelings of euphoria, exhilaration, and confidence
- Accelerated heart rate
- Increase in body temperature
- A burst of energy
- Dilated pupils
- Loss of appetite
- The urge to have sex

In high doses, cocaine will make the user feel extremely agitated, paranoid, and aggressive. Unpleasant physical effects include dizziness, hallucinations, nausea, vomiting, tremors, headache, and heart pain. The consequences of overdose include seizures, kidney failure, heart attack, or stroke.

Ecstasy is the common name for the illegal synthetic drug called Methylenedioxymethamphetamine (MDMA). It is both a stimulant and a hallucinogen, since it speeds up the workings of the central nervous system and alters the user's perception of reality. Teenagers like to use this as a mood enhancer at parties and nightclubs.

Ecstasy is usually swallowed as a tablet, but it can also come in powder form. This drug takes effect in around an hour, and might last for up to 32 hours.

When we are stressed out, the central nervous system readies us for physical action by creating particular physiological changes. These may include the release of adrenalin and other stress hormones. Key functions like heart rate and blood pressure may increase, redirecting the blood flow into the muscles and away from the stomach. Ecstasy prompts the brain to initiate this "fight or flight" response and the user feels refreshed by a burst of energy. Hallucinations of both sight and sound distort the user's experience of reality.

Generally some of the immediate effects of ecstasy include:

- Feelings of confidence, happiness, and benevolence
- Accelerated heart rate and breathing
- Rise in blood pressure
- Sweating and dehydration
- Nausea
- Jaw clenching and teeth grinding
- Loss of appetite
- Hallucinations
- An increased urge for sex
- Loss of inhibitions

Symptoms of overdose of ecstasy include a sharp rise in body temperature and blood pressure, dizziness, cramps, and vomiting. Ecstasy can cause death in a number of ways, including:

- Cardiac arrest
- Stroke
- Kidney failure
- Overheating and dehydration

Heroin is an illegal drug that is made from the resin or sap of the opium poppy. It is a central nervous system depressant, which means it slows down the workings of the brain and spinal cord. Heroin usually takes the form of granules or powder, and can be white, pink, or brown. It is usually injected, but some users snort or smoke it instead.

Heroin prompts the brain to release chemicals called endorphins, which are responsible for feelings of pleasure. Almost immediately upon injection, the user experiences a complete cessation of all physical pain and discomfort, and is flooded with intense pleasurable feelings. This comprehensive escape from reality into a warm, feel-good world is one powerful reason why heroin is so psychologically addictive.

Generally, some of the immediate effects of heroin include:

- A rush of pleasurable feelings
- Cessation of physical pain and discomfort
- Shallow breathing
- A drop in body temperature
- Sleepiness
- Narrowing of the pupils

A high dose of heroin can make the user feel sick and vomit. Constipation, for days or even weeks, is a common side effect of heroin use. The symptoms of overdose include:

- Irregular heartbeat
- Dangerously low body temperature
- Slowed breathing
- Unconsciousness
- Death

Using heroin on a regular basis can lead to significant health and lifestyle problems, including:

- Collapsed veins and skin abscesses
- Risk of contracting various blood borne viruses, such as HIV

and hepatitis, a blood poisoning from sharing needles and other injecting equipment.

- Chronic constipation
- Increased risk of contracting pneumonia and other lung problems
- Loss of sex drive
- Fertility problems
- Disturbances of the menstrual cycle for women
- Poor nutrition and reduced immunity
- Loss of relationships, career, and home and the need for the drug becomes all-consuming
- Increased risk of living a criminal lifestyle to support the habit
- Damage caused by dangerous fillers mixed with the heroin
- Risk of overdose

Are drugs such as the ones I've listed designed to "glorify God in your body?" Obviously, these drugs (and many others I haven't mentioned) damage and potentially destroy our bodies, which are temples of the Holy Spirit.

One more thought: Christians don't need drugs to solve their problems or to be happy. Christ gives us a sense of completion that cannot be found in drug-use. Romans 15:13 reads, "Now the God of hope fill you with all joy and peace in believing, that you may abound in hope through the power of the Holy Ghost."

Christ has given you the hope of eternal salvation. Why would want to ruin your life with drugs when you have so much for which to live?

If you already have an addiction to drugs, find help now. Talk to your parents. Talk to your preacher. Talk to your doctor. Contact the National Clearinghouse for Alcohol and Drug Information (1-800-729-6686) or the Higher Education Center for Alcohol and Other Drug Prevention (1-800-676-1730). The longer you wait, the more difficult it will be to stop.

Don't try to escape your problems through drugs. The only way to have true and lasting peace and joy is through Christ (Philippians 4:6, 7).

Questions:

1. Find some other passages in the Bible that show God's hatred for drunkenness.

2. Find an example of someone who became drunk in the Bible. Did any good come from it?

3. Find some scientific evidence which proves that drinking slows mental processing.

4. Find at least one Biblical example of someone who sinned in the same way their parent or parents sinned many years prior to that.

5. What is the legal blood/alcohol content level in your state? Does God's definition of "drunk" change from state to state?

6. Besides the destruction of the body, discuss how drugs impair and may disintegrate a young girl's system of morality. What other sins might she be more apt to commit if she is experimenting with drugs?

Projects

1. Research how big the problem of alcoholism is in America today. Present your research to the group at the next meeting.

2. Create a 20-page scrapbook consisting of current social problems in your town or state that result from the drinking of beverage alcohol. Present this scrapbook to your mentor.

3. Contact a Christian policeman in your area. Have him come to your next group meeting and discuss the relationship between the drinking of beverage alcohol and crime in your area. If this project is accomplished, it would count as one achieved project for each group member.

4. Write a three-page double spaced typed research paper on the dangers of nicotine. Remember to cite all of your sources. Submit the paper to your mentor.

5. Interview someone who has kicked the smoking habit. Ask questions about how long it took, what withdrawal symptoms he/she had, methods used, and advice for those who smoke and would like to stop. Bring a video copy of this interview and show it to your group at the next meeting.

6. Choose one of the drugs mentioned in this lesson and do a research paper on the dangers of that particular drug. Be sure to cite all sources. Submit the paper to your mentor.

7. Contact a D.A.R.E officer in your town. Have him come and speak to your group. This project counts as one achieved project for each member of the group.

8. Research drug abuse in the book of Genesis. Tell the story of drug abuse in the life of Noah and in the life of Lot. List some long-term effects of drug abuse that occurred in the descendents of these two men. Present this material to your group. (Hint: You will need to research the descendents of Ham, the Moabites, and the Ammonites.)

Works Cited

Most of the material used in Part I of this chapter was taken from Hannah Colley. *"Drinking"* in *Girl To Girl*. Ed. Laura Elliott. Huntsville, AL, Publishing Designs, 2005

"Drugs-some facts."
http://www.betterhealth.vic.gov.au/bhcv2/bhcarticles.nsf/pages/Drugs_some_facts?OpenDocument
"Cannabis (marijuana)"
http://www.betterhealth.vic.gov.au/bhcv2/bhcarticles.nsf/

pages/Cannabis
"Cocaine"
http://www.betterhealth.vic.gov.au/bhcv2/bhcarticles.nsf/
pages/Cocaine
"Ecstasy"
http://www.betterhealth.vic.gov.au/bhcv2/bhcarticles.nsf/
pages/Ecstasy
"Heroin"
http://www.betterhealth.vic.gov.au/bhcv2/bhcarticles.nsf/
pages/Heroin
 "Underage Drinking"
http://www.cdc.gov/alcohol/fact-sheets/underage-drinking.
htm
 "SIUC/Core Institute Survey Of Alcohol & Other Drug Use"
http://core.siu.edu/pdfs/report0911.pdf

CHAPTER ELEVEN:
Morality or Politics?

Part 1: Homosexuality

While the percentage of homosexuals in our nation is still extremely small in comparison to that of heterosexuals, our government and the people of America are becoming more and more influenced by the homosexual population and its activism.

Dictionary.com defines homosexuality as "a sexual attraction to (or sexual relations with) persons of the same sex."

You may think that homosexuality is a current issue. The legalization of homosexual marriage in America is a current issue, but homosexuality has been practiced for thousands of years. This part of the chapter will address the issue and carefully state the facts about a lifestyle that has recently become so widely accepted.

Did God Make Them That Way?

Many people believe that one simply can't help it if he/she is homosexual or "gay." Can homosexuality be explained by genetics? This question motivated the Human Genome Project, in which this very issue was analyzed.

In the study, educational institutions such as Baylor University, the Max Planck Institute, the Sanger Institute, Washington University in St. Louis, and others spent countless hours and millions of research dollars to analyze whether the two "sex" chromosomes, X and Y, contained any "gay gene." None was found.

To gain social acceptance, the assertion is frequently made that homosexuals deserve equal rights just as other minority groups and should not be punished for, or forbidden from, expressing their homosexuality. Often comparing their movement to the "civil rights" movements of racial minorities, homosexual activists are able to divert attention away from the behavior, and focus it on the rights.

You've heard the argument. It goes something like this: "Just as a person can't help being black, female, or Asian, I can't help being homosexual. We were all born this way, and so we should be treated equally." However, there is a striking difference between skin color or other such genetic traits and homosexuality. Homosexuals are not identified by a trait or a gene, but rather by their actions. Without the actions, they would be indistinguishable from all other people. If we somehow discovered that homosexuality was genetic, then one could conclude that those individuals are not morally responsible for being homosexual. However, that doesn't mean that they are not morally responsible for homosexual actions. Merely having the gene would not force one to act on that tendency. For example, if scientists discovered a "rape gene" in someone, we would never blame that person for possessing such a gene, but neither would we allow him to act on that rape disposition.

We all have different temptations. If you are attracted to someone of the same sex, it will be a greater temptation for you to abstain from homosexual activity. But remember, it works the same way with alcoholism or even an addiction to pornography. Do not believe the myth that, because someone is attracted to people of the same sex, that person is a homosexual. Rather, that person has a different kind of temptation than you may have. You may be struggling with an addiction to drugs, while that person has no such desire.

It has never been proven that homosexuality is genetic, and, most likely, never will be. My next point explains the unlikelihood of such a discovery.

What Does God Think About Homosexuality?

In Genesis 19 we read about two neighboring cities completely saturated with homosexuality. They were called Sodom and Gomorrah. We get the modern term, "sodomy" from Genesis 19, where we read about what occurred in these cities.

God became so disgusted with the sin of Sodom and Gomorrah that he planned to entirely destroy both cities (Genesis 18:20, 21).

God sent two angels to Sodom to warn Abraham's nephew, Lot, and his family about the destruction that was about to take place, so that they could escape the peril. Lot was the gatekeeper of the city (Genesis 19:1). Lot greeted the angels at the door and hospitably invited them to feast and rest at his house for the night. We have no evidence that Lot knew these men were angels. We can assume that he did not.

Before the angels had time to lie down and sleep, the men of Sodom yelled through the door of the house at Lot, begging him to bring out the two "men" that had entered his house, so that they could know them sexually (verse 4,5).

Lot begged the men to leave his guests alone, and even offered his virgin daughters to the men to satisfy their lusts (vs.7, 8). The wicked men would not leave, and when they were on the verge of breaking down the door, the angels pulled Lot into the house and struck every man outside the door with blindness. Even after they were blinded, they "wearied themselves to find the door (vs.9-11)." They were more concerned about committing fornication with the two angels than they were about losing their own sight.

The following day, God destroyed the cities with fire because of their wicked homosexuality.

Leviticus 18:22 reads, "You shall not lie with a man as a woman. It is an abomination."

Leviticus 20:13 reads, "If a man lies with a male as he lies with a woman, both of them have committed an abomination. They shall surely be put to death. Their blood shall be upon them."

We are no longer bound by the laws of the Old Testament because Christ died to establish the new law (Hebrews 10:1-12). However, in Old Testament passages such as the two above, we can see the crystal clear abomination God has for homosexuality. Now let's look at the New Testament.

Paul summarized the "unrighteous" and "ungodly" behavior of the Gentile nations when he declared in Romans 1:26-32:

"For this reason God gave them up to vile passions. For even their women exchanged the natural use for what is against nature. Likewise also the men, leaving the natural use of the woman, burned in their lust for one another, men with men committing what is shameful, and receiving in themselves the penalty of their error which was due. And even as they did not like to retain God in their knowledge, God gave them over to a debased mind, to do those things which are not fitting. ...who, knowing the righteous judgment of God, that those who practice such things are worthy of death, not only do the same but also approve of those who practice them."

God Himself tells us that homosexuality is "against nature," and that not only those who practice homosexuality are guilty, but those who approve of the people who practice it.

I Corinthians 6:9-11 shows us that homosexuals cannot enter the gates of heaven, "Do you not know that the unrighteous will not inherit the kingdom of God? Do not be deceived. Neither fornicators, nor idolaters, nor adulterers, nor homosexuals, nor sodomites, nor thieves, nor covetous, nor drunkards, nor revilers, nor extortioners, will inherit the kingdom of God. And such were some of you. But you were washed, but you were sanctified, but you were justified in the name of the Lord Jesus and by the Spirit of our God."

God has made it painfully clear for us. God hates homosexuality. Look at the words, "And such were some of you." This proves that homosexuals can not only be forgiven, but can stop being that way. Right here, we have Biblical evidence that a person can change his sexual orientation, and be forgiven of a past immoral lifestyle.

But Isn't It Unloving To Say Homosexuality Is Wrong?

Society screams that people who don't approve of homosexual unions are intolerant and unloving. You will probably sometimes be in the "out crowd" when you speak out against homosexuality. Some Christians seem to have forgotten Jesus' words in Matthew 5:10-11:

"Blessed are they which are persecuted for righteousness' sake: for theirs is the kingdom of heaven. Blessed are ye when men shall revile you and persecute you, and shall say all manner of evil against you falsely for my sake."

We have to remind ourselves to love the sinner but hate the sin. Just because we're opposed to that way of living doesn't mean we shouldn't reach out to those people and try to help them. They have souls just like we do. We shouldn't avoid talking to those people, but rather, we should be motivated to share the truth of God's word with them, and the forgiveness and happiness we can have in Christ.

Part 2: Abortion

How many times have you heard someone say, "It's her body! A woman should have the right to choose what she wants to do with it"? When you hear these words, the person speaking is probably talking about a woman's right to choose to abort her unborn child.

What Is Abortion?

To put it simply, abortion is intentionally taking the life of an unborn child. Every year in the United States, more than one million children are cut into pieces by abortion doctors. In 1973, our Supreme Court made the decision to legalize abortion-on-demand. Since then, some forty-three million babies have been slaughtered in America. More than 20% of all babies conceived in this country are killed before they ever see the light of day. More than one million teenage girls in the United States will become pregnant this year. Forty-eight percent of them will give birth, 11 percent will miscarry, and 41 percent will decide to take the baby's life through abortion.

There are many methods of abortion--all of them tragic--most of them excruciatingly painful for the baby. I've included a few of them below:

Saline Amniocentesis

This technique is used after 16 weeks of pregnancy. A concentrated salt solution is injected into the womb. The baby breathes in, swallowing the salt, and is poisoned. For over an hour, the baby writhes in pain as his skin is burned away until, finally, he dies. Two days later, the mother gives birth to a dead, burned, and shriveled baby.

Suction Curettage

In this procedure, a powerful vacuum with a knife-like edge on the tip is inserted into the uterus. The suction rips apart the baby's body, sucking out the blood, the amniotic fluids, the tissue, and all of the body parts, one by one.

Dilatation and Curettage

In this method, the cervix is dilated so a steel knife with a loop shape can be inserted into the uterus. The abortionist then uses this knife to scrape the wall of the uterus. This scraping cuts the unborn child into pieces and removes the child from the uterine wall.

Partial-Birth Abortion

This is a three-day procedure. During the first two days, the pregnant woman's cervix is anesthetized and dilated. On the day of the operation, the abortionist uses a sonogram to find the child's leg. Once the abortionist has a hold of a leg with forceps, the child is pulled through the birth canal until the whole child is delivered except for the head. The abortionist then stabs the baby at the base of his skull with scissors, and evacuates the contents of the skull so that it will be small enough to pull through the birth canal.

I know this is morbid and difficult to read. As I researched and listed these four out of many horrific methods of abortion, I had a hard time focusing on the computer screen through the tears I was crying. I am appalled that such a barbaric process is legal and accepted by many in our society. I can't imagine the amount of pain the tiny victims endure while they are being murdered. But it isn't just the baby that suffers because of abortion. Most doctors fail to mention the physical side effects and emotional torture that the mother of the unborn child suffers. Possible physical complications include uterine tears, cervix damage, infections, and increased risk of miscarriage in future pregnancies. Some women hemorrhage, endure severe infections, and go into shock. These are all horrible physical effects, but the worst suffering after an abortion is emotional. Within eight weeks after their abortions, one survey showed that 55 percent of the women expressed guilt, 44 percent complained about nervous disorders, 36 percent experienced sleep disturbances, and 31 percent regretted the decision to abort the baby.

Psychological effects include depression, loss of self-esteem, self-destructive behavior, sleep disorders, memory loss, sexual dysfunction, chronic problems with relationships, dramatic personality change, anxiety attacks, guilt, increased tendency toward violence, chronic crying, difficulty concentrating, flashbacks, loss of interest in previously enjoyed activities and people, and difficulty in bonding with later children.

Countless women could share stories about the terrifying ghosts of guilt they still live with years after the abortion occurred. One recent study showed that five years after mothers abort their babies, 96% of them believe the abortion had taken a human life.

What Does God Say About Abortion?

While the Bible does not directly address the practice of abortion, it provides so much relevant material to enable us to see God's will on the matter. In Zechariah 12:1, God is said to be not only the Creator of the heavens and the Earth, but also the one who "forms the spirit of man within him." So God is the giver of life. That alone makes human life sacred.

Psalm 139:13-16 reads, "For You have formed my inward parts;

You have covered me in my mother's womb. I will praise You, for I am fearfully and wonderfully made; marvelous are Your works, and that my soul knows very well. My frame was not hidden from You, when I was made in secret, and skillfully wrought in the lowest parts of the earth. Your eyes saw my substance, being yet unformed. And in Your book they all were written, the days fashioned for me, when as yet there were none of them."

David suggested that his development as a human being-his personhood-happened prior to his birth, while he was yet in his mother's womb.

Jeremiah 1:4-5 reads, "Then the word of the Lord came unto me, saying: 'Before I formed you in the womb I knew you; before you were born I sanctified you; and I ordained you a prophet to the nations'."

Isaiah said in Isaiah 49:1, "...The Lord has called me from the womb; from the matrix of my mother He has made mention of my name."

Let's look at a time when Mary, the mother of Jesus, went to pay a visit to Elizabeth, the mother of John the Baptist. Both women were pregnant at the time. Luke 1:39-44 reads,

"Now Mary arose in those days and went into the hill country with haste, to a city of Judah, and entered the house of Zacharias and greeted Elizabeth. And it happened, when Elizabeth heard the greeting of Mary, that the babe leaped in her womb; and Elizabeth was filled with the Holy Spirit. Then she spoke out with a loud voice and said, 'Blessed are you among women, and blessed is the fruit of your womb! But why is this granted to me, that the mother of my Lord should come to me? For indeed, as soon as the voice of your greeting sounded in my ears, the babe leaped in my womb for joy.'"

Notice that this pre-born baby of Elizabeth is referred to as a living human being. In fact, the "babe" used in verses 41 and 44 to refer to the pre-born John is the exact same term that is used in chapter two to refer to Jesus after His birth as he laid in the manger (Luke 2:12,16).

If abortion is not morally wrong, then why would it be wrong for Mary to abort her baby, Jesus-the divine Son of God? You may say, "Oh, that's different. God had a special plan for that child." But the Bible teaches that God has special plans for every human being. Every human life is precious to God. The remarkable resourceful potential for even one of the millions of tiny human minds extinguished by abortion may well have included a cure for cancer, or a U.S. president or an evangelist who could have reached thousands.

Our government has become increasingly inconsistent in reference to the value of life. Did you know that merely taking possession of an egg containing a pre-born American bald eagle results in a stiff fine and even prison time? Yet one can take a human child in its pre-born environment and not only murder that child, but also receive a government blessing to do so. So, pre-born eagles are of greater value to American civilization than pre-born humans! How did we, as a society, reach this bizarre conclusion?

A Real-Life Story

This story is true. The girl of whom I write will probably never know this story, even though it's about her. "Somebody is going to die." It was seventeen years ago. A middle-aged father stormed into my dad's counseling office with an indescribable vengeance. His young teenage daughter was pregnant. This father was obviously crazed as he said to my dad, "I'm gonna go get a gun and shoot that boy."

What a terrifying threat! And it wasn't just an idle threat. At that moment, Mr. Branson really had every intention of doing it! His daughter was pregnant and somebody was going to pay. My dad told this enraged man to have a seat and calm down. He then counseled with the man, making the man realize that he couldn't really mean what he was saying, and that taking the life of that young man was a senseless response to the situation.

After a while, the man calmed down and was willing to be more level-headed. Remember, he came in saying "someone is going to die." So option two: A much more thoughtful plan...a much simpler plan...one that is discreet, accepted, and convenient. Yes, this is the reasonable choice. "Okay," he said, "We'll just have an abortion."

The reasonable choice. The first option was to take the life of a young man by a quick hair-triggered blast. On the other hand, the reasonable choice could be one of the methods mentioned previously in this chapter. Thankfully, Mr. Branson was led to understand there in the quiet of that office that there was yet another choice. Eight months later his daughter gave birth to Christy, a beautiful, healthy baby girl.

You can imagine my Dad's sense of relief knowing that Christy's little life was allowed its right of passage from the womb. Not long after Christy's birth, though, my family moved away from the small town where Christy was growing up. We moved on to other Christys; to stand in human life chains; to write letters to editors in other towns; to be a voice wherever we could be heard for little lives that could not be heard.

But now let me tell you the rest of the story...

My family recently walked into a state Right to Life oratory competition in which my brother was speaking. My parents instantly recognized a family sitting in the back of the auditorium. As the contest progressed, a tall and very beautiful girl exited her row and made her way to the podium. She was eloquent. She was forceful for life. She was Christy. She gestured with her right hand as she passionately spoke for life. You know, that very hand could have been ripped off by forceps and removed from her mother's womb along with all of her limbs in a process called dilatation and evacuation.

As Christy made her final plea, she stepped forward with determination on healthy legs and steady feet.   Remember the "reasonable choice?" Some babies today whose parents opt for the "reasonable choice" have tiny healthy legs and feet with tiny toes that have already wiggled for the first time in the air which we all breathe. Yes, the little baby's body all except the head is already stretching and feeling and awakening outside the womb, when suddenly its tiny body is turned so that it can be stabbed at the base of its little skull and its head collapses.

We must educate in the quiet rooms of counsel and in public arenas for all of the Christys. "Somebody has to die," he said. Certainly taking the life of the teenage boy was a senseless and violent option. Was option number two a reasonable choice? Are the methods of abortion any less violent? Both options would have stopped a beating heart. Both options would have snuffed out great potential. Both options would have left behind great ghosts of guilt. But there is one principle difference.

The case of the pistol's quick blast would have ended up in a court of law, where a grave penalty would have been exacted for his murder. But the tiny life would never have been defended. It would never have been heard. But I heard Christy, and the indelible image of her vibrant voice for life will always be with me.

Christy doesn't know what my father knows, and he will never tell her. She doesn't know that her tiny life once hung in the balance. She doesn't know that someone educated, interceded, and actually pleaded on her behalf. On that day, the choice was made. But there are Christys whose lives are in danger every day in America. It is for them that we must continue the fight to educate and legislate for life...the really reasonable choice.

Questions:

1. Find recent statistics on the number of practicing homosexuals in our country.

2. What words describe homosexuality in Leviticus 18:22-30? Look up the word "abomination" and define it.

3. What was the punishment for homosexuality found in Leviticus 20:13?

4. What passage in the New Testament describes lesbianism?

5. What is the etymology of the word "sodomy?"

6. Find out what the Greek word is for "babe" in Luke 1:41,44 and in Luke 2:12,16.

7. Make a list of things teenage girls can do in their communities to increase awareness of the taking of innocent human life and to prevent it.

Projects

1. Go to www.apologeticspress.org and research genetics and

homosexuality. Write a research paper using this and other sources to show that homosexuality has not been proven to be genetic. Submit this to your mentor.

2. Memorize Leviticus 18:22-30, Leviticus 20:13, Romans 1:26-32, and I Corinthians 6:9-11. Quote these to your mentor.

3. Research your state laws regarding homosexual unions. Bring these to your next meeting and discuss whether this legislation is good or if it needs revising.

4. Find a girl or woman in your community or school who is willing to debate the following proposition: Affirmative: People who practice homosexuality without repentance will be eternally lost. Negative: People who practice homosexuality without repentance will not be eternally lost. Form a debate team from the members of your GIFTS group and debate this before a group of women from your congregation or community. Have your mentor or minister formulate a list of rules for the debate.

5. Research the various methods of abortions performed today. Begin at www.nrlc.org/abortion and write a research paper to submit to your mentor on this topic.

6. Contact an attorney and find out if the word "sodomy" is still used in your state's written laws. If so, bring a list of laws containing the word "sodomy" to share with your GIFTS group.

7. Research the Partial Birth Abortion laws in your state. Document the history of this method in your state and bring this documentation to your GIFTS mentor.

8. Prepare a speech about the after-effects of abortion on women. Present this speech to your GIFTS group.

9. Research a woman named Norma McCorvey, who was once called

"Jane Roe." Write the story of how this woman was involved in Roe vs. Wade and about how that in recent years, this woman has changed her position on abortion. Read this story to your GIFTS group.

10. Write a letter to the editor of your local newspaper expressing your views on abortion or homosexuality. Have your mentor proofread and offer suggestions before sending it in.

11. Write letters to the state legislators who represent your district and ask them to vote pro-life. Do the same for the national legislators who represent your state.

Works Cited

"'This is the Way God Made Me.'-A Scientific Examination of Homosexuality and the 'Gay Gene.'" August 2004
http://www.apologeticspress.org/apcontent.aspx?category=11&article=1388

"An Investigation of the Biblical Evidence Against Homosexuality." September 2004
http://www.apologeticspress.org/articles/2577

"Abortion: Some Medical Facts"
http://www.nrlc.org/abortion/ASMF/asmf.html

CHAPTER TWELVE:
Here and Now Evangelism

Mark 16:15 reads, "...Go ye into all the world and preach the gospel to every creature."

How can "go into all the world" apply to me? I'm just a teenager! Have you ever thought this?

Don't let yourself fall into the mindset that says, "I'm too young to be evangelistic now." We have to remember that we, as teenagers, have more opportunities to influence others than most people in the world do. Just because you may not be able to fly to Africa and help establish a church right now doesn't mean you can't be spreading the good news of the gospel in your own world. Your peers are more impressionable right now than they will ever be. Don't let your middle and high school years go by without reaching out to your friends with the truth of God's Word.

Foreign missions is a wonderful, and faith strengthening passion of many people, and we need more people to get involved. However, traveling to teach in foreign countries is not the most difficult kind of mission work. The most difficult mission fields are your school, your neighborhood, your workplace, and the places where you hang out. It's easier to talk to someone in a foreign country about the Lord because even if they reject the gospel and treat you unkindly, it doesn't really matter, because you'll probably never see them again! But it's different here at home. When we think about talking to people in our very own social circles, our palms get sweaty. Our stomachs start to feel funny. But think about it: Who do you think makes our palms sweaty, puts butterflies in our stomachs, and makes our hearts skip a beat? It's definitely not the Lord. It's the devil, and he's the most difficult barrier of all. Don't let him get in your way of "going into all the world."

We have to force our mouths open for the Lord. Each time you make yourself speak up for God, it's like taking a sledge hammer to those barriers that make you so afraid to mention His name. It only takes a few seconds to say, "Would you like to study the Bible with me sometime?" or "How about going to the youth devo with me tonight?" But those few seconds can mean the difference between an eternity in heaven or hell.

At the time I was writing this chapter, I was working at a fast food restaurant with several other teenagers. I was constantly amazed that even though they were so saturated with the sinful ways of the world, they were fascinated every time I talked about my faith. To have any sense of moral boundaries seems completely foreign to them. My teenage friends who were dealing with unwanted pregnancy, drug addictions, and horrible relationship issues were beginning to see that people who love and obey the Lord don't have to deal with these things.

So, what can we, as teenage girls, do to spread the gospel?

Open Doors

The first step to being evangelistic is to realize that every person has a soul. We have to constantly remind ourselves that it's not just a friend, not just a teacher, not just the boy who sits behind you in biology class, not just the mailman, not just the librarian—but a soul. When we're with our girlfriends, it's so easy to talk about who cuts our hair, the kinds of cars we drive, and our favorite places to shop. We tend to focus on all of these earthly things, while we forget that they have souls.

However, walking up to a stranger and saying "Hello. Would you like to study the Bible with me?" is usually not the best way to go about sharing Christ with people. We have to form relationships with people and show them the peace and kindness that dwells in the life of every faithful Christian. This is friendship evangelism.

I will not dispute the old saying, "I'd rather see a sermon than hear one any day." We cannot lead anyone to Christ if we aren't living the Christian life. However, we can't teach by example alone. A person can't learn God's plan for salvation by watching the way we live. We have to open our mouths and say something. But we don't have to start out with, "Would you study the Bible with me?" There are so many little ways that we can show Christ's love every day. When you give your friends birthday gifts or get-well care baskets, include Bible tracts or tapes with sermons about the church and about salvation. Before you leave a restaurant, try leaving a little flyer on the table inviting your waiter to worship.

My family has become acquainted with a waiter at a Mexican restaurant where we eat almost every Sunday. One day, my mom asked him if he would be interested participating in a Spanish Bible correspondence course. He immediately agreed, and is currently studying nightly through that course. When your friends are going through a rough time, let them know that you're praying for them daily. If you continue showing little acts of faith, your friends will want to know more about what makes you the way you are. If you keep developing those relationships in which you can show Christ's love, God will give you opportunities to share the truth with people.

Once we reach the point of being able to say, "Let's study the Bible together," how can we show people how to get to heaven?

Open Bible

How do we teach someone the plan of salvation? There are different ways to go about doing this. I've included my favorite. This is my adaptation of a study developed by the late Arnold Wright, who was elder at the West Huntsville Church of Christ in Huntsville, Alabama. I feel that it is important to have at least one specific guide in mind to use when teaching someone the gospel. Mark your Bible so that you will always be ready to share this wonderful gift God has offered us.

Soul Survivor's Guide

Begin by discussing God's plan for man's salvation as it unfolded in the patriarchal age; the fact that God called people to obey him through the fathers even in that era. Then discuss God's first written law, the Mosaic age, and the system of cleansing for the Jews in that era. Then point out that since the death of Christ, God has called his people by a new name. What is that new name?

Isaiah 62:2 says, "And the Gentiles shall see thy righteousness, and all kings thy glory: and thou shalt be called by a new name, which the mouth of the LORD shall name." What is that new name?

Acts 11:26 says, "And when he had found him, he brought him unto Antioch. And it came to pass, that a whole year they assembled themselves with the church, and taught much people. And the disciples were called Christians first in Antioch."

God kept that promise. Are you a Christian? How did you become a Christian? Have the person detail her "salvation experience" if she has "been saved". Write this down. Next, discuss the truth that a person must be in Christ in order to be redeemed or saved.

Ephesians1:3,7, "Blessed be the God and Father of our Lord Jesus Christ, who hath blessed us with all spiritual blessings in heavenly places in Christ: In whom we have redemption through his blood, the forgiveness of sins, according to the riches of his grace."

Here you are beginning to make a list of the blessings that are only found IN CHRIST. Have the person mentally if not literally keep a note of the things that can occur only IN CHRIST. (Here are a number of passages from which to choose to list these blessings: II Timothy 2:1; Ephesians 2:6, 10, 12, 13; II Corinthians 5:17; Romans 3:24; Romans8:1; I Thessalonians4:16)

Next, launch a study of verses that tell how to get IN CHRIST. In these verses notice the difference in the passages that say we do something UNTO salvation and those that say we do something INTO Christ.

John 8:24; John 14:6, "I said therefore unto you, that ye shall die in your sins: for if ye believe not that I am he, ye shall die in your sins. Jesus saith unto him, I am the way, the truth, and the life: no man cometh unto the Father, but by me." (Additional verses if needed for belief include

Hebrews 11:6; Romans10:17; James 1:21-25)

Luke 13:3, "I tell you, Nay: but, except ye repent, ye shall all likewise perish."

Acts 26:18, "To open their eyes, and to turn them from darkness to light, and from the power of Satan unto God, that they may receive forgiveness of sins, and inheritance among them which are sanctified by faith that is in me."

The definition of repentance is TURNING. Additional verses for repentance if needed: Acts 17:30; II Corinthians 7:10; II Peter 3:9. This is the point at which I ask what kinds of things might have to be changed or sacrificed to live for Christ. I recall Romans 8:1 at this juncture and talk about the two conditions there for NOT being condemned. They are (1) being IN CHRIST and (2) walking not after the flesh, but after the Spirit. Then I define this pure walk plainly and practically using the fruit of the spirit from Galatians 5:19-25. This is a great time to talk about faithfulness in all aspects of daily living.

Romans 10:10; Acts 8:37- "For with the heart man believeth unto righteousness; and with the mouth confession is made unto salvation."

"And Philip said, If thou believest with all thine heart, thou mayest. And he answered and said, I believe that Jesus Christ is the Son of God."

WHAT did he confess? Additional passage for confession if needed: Matthew 10:32. Notice the UNTO in Romans 10:10.

Here are the clinchers in the IN CHRIST study: Romans 6:1-5, "What shall we say then? Shall we continue in sin, that grace may abound? God forbid. How shall we, that are dead to sin, live any longer therein? Know ye not, that so many of us as were baptized into Jesus Christ were baptized into his death? Therefore we are buried with him by baptism into death: that like as Christ was raised up from the dead by the glory of the Father, even so we also should walk in newness of life. For if we have been planted together in the likeness of his death, we shall be also in the likeness of his resurrection."

Galatians 3:27, "For as many of you as have been baptized into Christ have put on Christ."

Additional powerful passages about the nature and purpose of baptism are Mark 16:16, Acts 2:38, Acts 22:16 and I Peter 3:21.

At this point, I usually try to illustrate the difference between being outside the room and inside the room. At what point did I get IN the room? When I was knocking at the door was I IN? Only when I had passed through the doorway did I get IN the room. Baptism is the door! I usually emphasize also according to Romans 6 and Galatians 3 that baptism is the point at which I contact the death without which there is NO remission (Hebrews 9:22). This is also the point at which to refute infant baptism, a baptism which would precede or preclude repentance, and sprinkling, a baptism in which the death of Christ is not mirrored or met.

The obvious question at this juncture is either "Are you a New Testament Christian?" or "Don't You want to be a Christian?" If you wrote down earlier a "salvation experience" this is the time to determine if that experience put the subject in Christ.

Open-Ended

The most important thing we have to tell ourselves is "never give up." Just because a person seems disinterested now doesn't mean we can stop doing all that we can to influence him. We have to continue to strive to set the best example possible and to pray daily for that person, remembering that, although the person isn't receptive now, we can continue to plant seeds that may grow later in that person's life. Someday that person may remember the things you've said and come to you to learn more, and you may be able to teach that person the gospel.

There's nothing like the feeling a Christian gets when she witnesses a person she has taught put on Christ in baptism. It is amazing and wonderful. But what happens after that? It's easy to say, "Well, I've converted that person, so I don't have to worry about her anymore." But that person you've converted is a babe in Christ, and she needs encouragement now more than ever. Pay attention to her attendance patterns at worship, and help her to be faithful. Make sure you pray for her everyday, and never pass up an opportunity to study the Bible with her. There is never a point at which we can say, "I'm finished." We can't stop working for the Lord until He comes to take us home.

I'd like to share with you a poem which my mother, Cindy Colley, wrote about remembering that every person has a soul:

We'd walk to the corner together,
Eat M&M's and wait for the bus.
I remember she'd always stick up for me
When Tad Smith would make fun of us.

We played for the Rascals together.
She knew how to clean up the bases.
She pitched. I was catcher. We had secret signals.
I'd laugh when she made silly faces.

We'd share a shake in the food court
When her mom drove us to the mall.
We'd pretend not to notice the boys when they passed;
By now Tad was not bad at all.

I was better with numbers.
We'd painstakingly work each equation.
She grabbed me and hugged me, then straightened my cap
When we lined up for our graduation.

So many memories of glad times;
So warm was the laughter and fun.
Where did the years go when we left that place?
How could our lives here be done?

We went to the Judgment together,
Once more we were standing in line.
I had one more chance to look into the face
Of this wonderful old friend of mine.

It spoke of the bus stop, the ball field, the school;
Of math class, the mall, and the show.
In all of these times I never had told her
Of this one final place we would go.

Just one more day at the bus stop,
Or shopping and sharing a shake;
Just one more test for eleventh grade trig;
One more, that's all it would take.

I'd be sure this time not to miss them;
Those everyday chances to show
The Christ of the cross, His hope for the lost,
This time I would tell her I know.
But there's no going back. It's all over.
A whispered "goodbye," and it's severed;
A friendship so strong, yet it ended so wrong.
It's all over forever and ever.

You don't have to wait until the next youth group mission trip to reach out to lost souls. Every single day should be a mission trip for Christians. So, go ahead! Tear the barriers down. Always remember II Timothy 1:7, "...God has not given us a spirit of fear, but of power and of love..."

Questions:

1. Find at least three scriptures teaching us to be evangelistic.

2. Why are friends harder to teach than strangers?

3. What are some good ways we can be evangelistic in our communities?

4. Can a person go to heaven if she has never taught someone the gospel?

5. How can James 4:17 apply to sharing what we know about God's plan for salvation?

6. Find a scripture which describes how we should confront others about their spiritual well-being (hint: with anger or meekness?).

Projects

1. Think of all the people you know who are lost, and narrow this list down to three people who would be the most likely to respond to the good news of Christ. Pray for each of those three people daily for one month. Choose one of those people who will be your main focus. Ask this person to study the Bible with you. Invite him/her to go to worship with you. Write him/her letters of encouragement including uplifting Bible verses. Go out of your way to show kindness to this person. Do everything you can to influence this person for good. Pray for opportunities, and God will give them to you.

2. Organize a door-knocking day for your youth group. Choose a specific area in your town that you are going to cover. If you have a youth minister, ask him to help you with this project. At each door, invite the person to worship with you at your congregation, and leave information about the church in case she would like to contact the preacher to set up a Bible study. If each person in your group participates in this effort, each member can count this as one of her projects.

3. Find a faithful overseas missionary to support on your own. You might need to ask the elders of your congregation about who would be a good choice. Commit to pray for this person daily and to write a letter of encouragement to this missionary every month for a year. Ask your "adopted missionary" what you can do to help the people where he is working. Save some of your money to send for this effort. Share any letters you receive from your missionary with your group.

4. Ask your elders to consider allowing you to go to a foreign or US mission trip. Raise your own funds for this effort.

5. Make a list of things (kindnesses) you can do to begin the process of teaching a friend. List at least twenty things. Do three of these before the next class session.

6. Develop your own study guide to share the gospel. Bring a typed

copy to the next meeting for each girl.

7. Buy a small dry erase board for your room. On this board, list all people you hope to influence from Christ and pray daily for each of these by name for one month.

8. Host a missions forum at your church building for any area elders or missionaries to discuss their various works with your youth group. Have your elders approve all guest speakers.

CHAPTER THIRTEEN:
The Gift Exchange

If you've made it to this chapter, you've studied many aspects of faithful Christian living. Hopefully, reading this book has been a growth experience for you, helping you to examine yourself and what you can do to strengthen your relationship with Christ. Studying for, researching for, and writing this book has definitely stretched my personal faith in ways I can't even describe.

When we look at the characteristics of a faithful Christian, as were discussed in this book, it's easy to become overwhelmed and say, "I don't know if I can do this by myself." Thanks be to God, we don't have to. Our brothers and sisters in Christ are there to be leaned on, bearing our burdens with us (Galatians 6:2).

Nobody said that Christianity would be easy. In fact, Paul, by inspiration, said in II Timothy 3:12, "...all that will live godly in Christ Jesus will suffer persecution."

That verse means that if I am truly doing my very best to be a faithful Christian, I will have to suffer for it. God knew that we would all struggle as Christians. That's why he designed the church as a congregational system—so that we would always have each other when we need support.

This chapter will suggest ways that we can edify our brothers and sisters in Christ, and support each other as we strive to make it to heaven together.

Be Family

Why do you think God identifies Christians as brothers and sisters? The reason is that He wants us to love each other and depend on each other much like we love and depend on our earthly families.

Think about it. Who are some of the first people you call when you're in trouble? Your family! A family love should always be an unconditional love. Your family is a group of people who knows you--inside and out--and loves you just the same. Whenever I'm in any kind of crisis, my family is always there to back me up and help me get through it.

God wants us to have this kind of relationship with our brothers and sisters in Christ.

Jesus said in Matthew 12:50, "For whosoever shall do the will of my Father which is in heaven, the same is my brother, and sister, and mother."

Our responsibility as Christian girls is to be the best, most supportive sisters we can be.

Be Forgiving

Romans 12 immerses the reader with information on how we are to be truly encouraging to others. One of the main things Paul stresses in this chapter is stated in verses 19-21:

"Dearly beloved, avenge not yourselves, but rather give place unto wrath: for it is written, Vengeance is mine; I will repay, saith the Lord. Therefore if thine enemy hunger, feed him; if he thirst, give him drink: for in so doing thou shalt reap coals of fire on his head. Be not overcome of evil, but overcome evil with good."

Society has given us the message which says, "Don't get mad; get even." But God gives us a different message. We are commanded to unfailingly forgive (Matthew 18:21, 22); always turning the other cheek (Matthew 5:39).

We have an abundant amount of Biblical evidence that God is pretty serious about forgiveness. In Matthew 6, Jesus taught us how we are to pray. Notice how He seems to dwell on forgiveness. After He's finished praying, he goes on to elaborate on what He said earlier in the prayer. Verses 12-15 reads, "And forgive us our debts, as we forgive our debtors. And lead us not into temptation, but deliver us from the evil one. For thine is the kingdom, and the power, and the glory, for ever. Amen. **For if ye forgive men their trespasses, your heavenly Father will also forgive you: But if ye forgive not men their trespasses, neither will your Father forgive your trespasses."**

According to verse 15, if we aren't willing to forgive other people, God will refuse to forgive us.

All Christians make mistakes. We have to love each other enough to always be ready to forgive.

Be Forever

The main thing we have to remember in reference to our Christian family is that we aren't just forming relationships so that we'll have a good life here on earth. We're preparing for an eternity in heaven together. If we can't get along with each other here on earth, what makes you think God's going to allow you to go on bickering in heaven? Yes, we're different. Yes, we have different personalities. But we have no excuse for being the cause of strife within the body of Christ.

We need to strive to be like Barnabas. Every time we read about Barnabas, he was encouraging someone. His very name means "son of exhortation." It was Barnabas who stood up for Paul when the doubting Jewish Christians questioned the genuineness of Paul's conversion (Acts 9:27). It was Barnabas who believed in young John Mark when Paul believed John Mark wasn't mature enough to accompany them on a missionary journey (Acts 15). Because of Barnabas' constant encouragement, John Mark went on to accomplish great things.

Practical Suggestions

Be friendly! Christians should be easy to recognize simply by the smiles that they wear. As a Christian, you should be the very best kind of friend that anyone could want. Be there for each other at all times.

Always pray for each other. Try arranging a weekly prayer meeting with two or three other Christian girls. At that time, discuss the issues you're facing, and pray for those specific issues together.

Write notes! Send encouraging notes to your Christian brothers and sisters frequently, reminding them that you are thinking and praying for them.

When one of your Christian sisters is headed in the wrong direction spiritually, don't ignore the issue. Remember that her salvation is at risk, and talk to her about it. Encourage the other teenage girls of your congregation to try to help her, as well.

I hope you've enjoyed this study. Don't let the GIFTS program be the extent of your spiritual activities. Let this be the starting point.

May God bless you as you strive to study and grow stronger in your faith. I'll be keeping you in my prayers. I hope to see you in heaven one day. Never give up!

Questions:

1. List 10 New Testament scriptures that use the term brother or sister to refer to our family in Christ.

2. What are some specific ways that we can encourage our Christian sisters?

3. List at least 3 examples of Bible characters who were encouraging people.

4. Why do you think God felt so strongly about us being forgiving people?

5. Could it have anything to do with how much He's forgiven us?

6. Find at least three verses which instruct us on how we are to treat our Christian family.

7. What is something good that John Mark did after his missionary journeys with Paul and Barnabas?

8. List 3 scriptures proving that all Christians suffer.

9. To whom does vengeance belong?

10. With what spirit should we approach a sister who is involved in sin (Galatians 6:1)?

11. Find a verse that says we should be friendly.

Projects

1. Write an essay on encouragement. Be sure to include scripture. Submit this to your mentor.

2. Send at least 3 notes of encouragement in the mail every week for one month.

3. Organize a weekly prayer meeting to discuss and pray about current issues you're facing. Do this for one month. As many girls in your group as would like may participate. Those who attend every week may count this as one of their projects.

4. Each Sunday for one month, have your mentor assign each of you a different widow to sit beside during worship. If possible, sit with a different widow each Sunday. Not only will you make someone's day by this gesture, but you will probably grow through the relationships you're forming with the older members of your congregation.

5. Find a person who has mistreated you or wrongfully accused you. "Heap coals of fire" on her head (Proverbs 25:21, 22). Report to your

group about what you did. Make sure your report is not gossip or ill treatment of this person. Find every New Testament passage about Barnabas. Prepare a five-minute lesson from these passages. Present this lesson to your GIFTS group at the next meeting.

6. Read the book *"My Sister's Keeper"* edited by Kerry Duke. This book can be ordered from:

> Tennessee Bible College Bookstore
> P.O. Box 865
> Cookeville, Tennessee
> 38503-0865

7. Have a pizza party where each girl brings a plate of homemade cookies and a note describing how this study has helped her. Swap plates of cookies and notes.

8. Email the author of GIFTS at HGISELBACH@gmail.com and let her know what you liked about the study and what you think could be improved and how. Your suggestions will be seriously considered.

Notes

Notes

Notes

Notes

Notes